Brief Contents

How to Use
The Little Pearson Handbook

If you want a quick overview of what's in this book, you can look at the Brief Contents on p. i.

If you see a chapter that interests you in the Brief Contents, you can go to the page number listed or turn to the appropriate part opening page for a detailed list of the contents of that part of the book.

If you want to know more about what's in a particular chapter or part, then you can also look at the full Contents on pages vii–ix.

If you want to know where to find help for a very specific issue or if you need to look up a particular term, then you can refer to the Index on page 287.

If you need help starting your research paper, refer to "Research Map: Conducting Research" at the beginning of Part 2.

If you want information about MLA, APA, CMS, CSE, or IEEE documentation styles for research writing, turn to the first page of the appropriate chapter in Part 3. You will find a complete index of sample citations for each documentation style.

You will also find more help at the back of this book:
- A list of Common Errors of grammar, punctuation, and mechanics that many writers make
- A Revision Guide of editing and proofreading symbols
- A Glossary with basic grammatical and usage terms

WRITING ACROSS THE CURRICULUM

You can quickly locate information related to writing across the curriculum by using the list below. In addition to resources for specific disciplines, this page highlights topics that cross disciplines or extend to public and professional contents.

Writing in the Humanities

2a	Become a critical reader
5b	Write a scholarly essay in the humanities
5f	Write an essay exam
8b	Present effectively
10c	Finding print sources in the humanities
10e-g	Finding online sources in the humanities
14a-k	MLA documentation
14l-m	Sample MLA research paper and works-cited page
16a-d	CMS (Chicago) documentation
16e	Sample CMS research paper and references

Writing in the Social Sciences and Education

5a	Write an observation
5f	Write an essay exam
8b	Present effectively
10c	Finding print sources in the social sciences
10e-g	Finding online sources in the social sciences
15a-f	APA documentation
15g	Sample APA research paper and references
19a	Recognize active and passive voice

Writing in the Sciences

5a	Write an observation
5c	Write a scholarly essay in nursing
5e	Write a lab report
8b	Present effectively
10c	Finding print sources in the sciences
10e-g	Finding online sources in the sciences
10g	Finding visual sources in the sciences
17a-d	CSE documentation
19a	Recognize active and passive voice

Writing in Engineering

5d	Write an engineering report
8b	Present effectively
10e-g	Finding sources online
18a-d	IEEE documentation
19a	Recognize active and passive voice
21	Write with emphasis

Writing in the World

2b	Become a critical viewer
6a	Compose blogs and discussion posts
6b	Create multimedia projects
8a	Design basics
8b	Present effectively
20	Write concisely
21	Write with emphasis
22b	Be aware of levels of formality

LESTER FAIGLEY

University of
Texas at Austin

ROGER GRAVES

University of
Alberta

HEATHER GRAVES

University of
Alberta

THIRD
CANADIAN
EDITION

THE LITTLE
PEARSON
HANDBOOK

PEARSON

Toronto

Vice-President, CMPS: Gary Bennett
Editorial Director: Claudine O'Donnell
Acquisitions Editor: David LeGallais
Marketing Manager: Jennifer Sutton
Program Manager: Laura Pratt
Project Manager: Andrea Falkenberg
Developmental Editor: Leona Burlew
Media Editor: Lila Campbell
Media Developer: Tiffany Palmer

Production Services: Cenveo® Publisher
Services
Permissions Project Manager: Sue Petrykewycz
Photo Permissions Research: Nazveena Begum
Syed, Lumina Datamatics Inc.
Text Permissions Research: Mark Schaefer,
Lumina Datamatics Inc.
Cover Designer: Anthony Leung
Cover Image: Theseamuss/Fotolia Image Bank

10 9 8 7 6 5 4 3 2 1 DOC

Library and Archives Canada Cataloguing in Publication
Faigley, Lester, 1947–
[Little Penguin handbook]
    The little Pearson handbook / Lester Faigley (University of Texas at Austin), Roger Graves (University of Alberta), Heather Graves (University of Alberta).—Third Canadian edition.

Includes index.
    Revision of: The little Penguin handbook / Lester Faigley, Roger Graves, Heather Graves.—2nd Canadian ed. —Toronto : Pearson, ©2013.
ISBN 978-0-205-96652-3 (pbk.)

    1. English language—Rhetoric—Handbooks, manuals, etc. 2. English language—Grammar—Handbooks, manuals, etc. 3. Report writing—Handbooks, manuals, etc. I. Graves, Heather, 1958–, author II. Graves, Roger, 1957–, author III. Title.

PE1408.F333 2015   808'.042   C2015-900769-0

ISBN 978-0-205-96652-3

Contents

PART

6 Punctuation and Mechanics

Preface

The third Canadian edition of *The Little Pearson Handbook* responds to the need for a compact resource for students who must write assignments in a variety of courses but who are probably not in a writing or composition class—which turns out to be a category that covers almost all students! The focus of nonwriting courses is necessarily on the discipline itself that students are studying; the concise format of *The Little Pearson Handbook* helps keep the focus on the discipline while at the same time providing enough support to enable students to write their assignments well.

Recent research by the authors of *The Little Pearson Handbook* shows that many Canadian institutions require students to prepare writing assignments in *every course* that these institutions offer, and well over 80 percent of courses require students to write at least one assignment. In many programs students write more than sixty assignments in their academic careers. If students are to write as well as they possibly can, they need a guide. *The Little Pearson Handbook* is that guide.

The handbook gives students the information they need in as compact a format as possible. Each chapter begins with a new QuickTake or pointform summary of the material that follows; lists and tables highlight key information in each chapter. Examples appear for many of the kinds of document that students will encounter in their academic careers. *The Little Pearson Handbook* also provides answers to questions that students most frequently ask as they work through the process of writing.

To support students as they write, this edition of *The Little Pearson Handbook* is organized around the writing processes most frequently used to produce academic writing. Part 1 provides advice about how to get started on an assignment: how to read academic texts critically; how to plan an assignment; and how to draft a coherent document. New chapters guide students on how to write academic arguments (Chapter 4) and how to write for online courses (Chapter 6).

Part 2 provides more elaborate and detailed advice on the writing process in the context of researched assignments. Students will learn how to locate important sources in both physical and online libraries, and how to evaluate and cite those sources effectively. They will also find guidance on how to avoid plagiarism by summarizing and paraphrasing correctly and how to avoid "patch" plagiarism. Part 3 teaches students a clear, concise, and correct process for giving credit according to the rules of several disciplines when they conduct their research. Part 4 offers succinct advice about writing style and language, and Parts 5 and 6 focus on the rules for grammar, punctuation, and mechanics.

The Little Pearson Handbook provides a comprehensive amount of advice about writing in a distinctly compact format. It is a key resource that all post-secondary students need to support their development as writers.

ROGER GRAVES AND HEATHER GRAVES

MyWritingLab (www.mywritinglab.com)

MyWritingLab Where practice, application, and demonstration meet to improve writing. MyWritingLab, a complete online learning program, provides additional resources and effective practice exercises for developing writers. MyWritingLab accelerates learning through layered assessment and a personalized learning path. With over eight thousand exercises and immediate feedback to answers, the integrated learning aids of MyWritingLab reinforce learning throughout the semester.

PART 1

Composing

1 | Thinking as a Writer

QUICKTAKE

- Understand the process of communication (see below)
- Know how to get readers to take you seriously (see pp. 3–4)

1a   Four Keys to Communication

The process of communication requires the interaction of three essential elements: the **writer** (or speaker), the **audience**, and the **subject**. Figure 1.1 represents these elements as a rhetorical triangle.

Writer, subject, and audience are each necessary to communicate. These three elements affect each other. Writers adjust their presentation of a subject in response to the reader (think of how speaking to a friend differs from speaking to your instructor). Readers (such as instructors) also adjust to writers, making decisions about the significance of what they are reading as they read. The subject or topic you are writing about can also affect what you decide to say to an audience based on your familiarity with the topic.

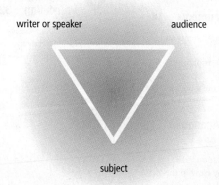

Figure 1.1   The rhetorical triangle

Context also affects communication. Particular subjects have historical dimensions for particular audiences. Any discussion of language laws in Quebec will be read and understood differently by audiences within Quebec and audiences in, say, Alberta or Saskatchewan. The writer, the reader, and the subject each bring histories to a particular rhetorical situation that affect what the writer can and should say. People who know how to communicate effectively use those histories to their advantage. They realize that others have written about the topic before them and they are entering an ongoing conversation.

1b Your Instructor as Audience

In post-secondary education, over 90 percent of the assignments you write will be for readers whom you know directly, such as your classmates and your instructors. In the workplace you may not have met whoever is going to read your report, memo, or résumé. Ask yourself who will read your writing and think about what kind of information you need to provide to engage them.

Understand your audience

1. Who will read what you write?
2. How much does the instructor know about your topic? Does the instructor want you to define key terms or concepts to show you know them?
3. What aspect of your treatment of the topic will the instructor find interesting?
4. What does the instructor want to see you do in this assignment: compare, synthesize, evaluate?

1c Your Credibility as a Writer

Most student writers have to demonstrate to their instructors that they have done the course readings and research. They must also show that they understand the readings and research and have summarized those materials accurately.

Build your credibility

1. How can you show your knowledge of your subject? Do you need to do research? Can you explain complex ideas in simple terms?
2. How do you demonstrate that you understand your readers' needs? Can you anticipate and respond to objections or questions?
3. To build your credibility, can you cite experts on the subject? Should you include opposing viewpoints to show you are fair?
4. The appearance, accuracy, and clarity of your writing builds your credibility; how can you improve these aspects of your writing?

2 | Reading Academic Texts

QUICKTAKE

- Ask questions while you read (see below)
- Analyze visual texts (see p. 6)

2a Become a Critical Reader

You can become a more effective critical reader if you have a set of strategies and use them while you read.

Preview

No subject is ever completely new; it is likely that many people have written and talked about the subject before. Begin by asking the following questions:

- Who wrote this material?
- Where did it first appear? In a book, newspaper, journal, or online?

- What is the issue being discussed?
- What stand does the writer take on the issue?
- What have others writing on this topic said about it?
- Why was it written?

Summarize

Make sure you understand exactly what is at issue. Circle any words or references that you don't know and look them up. Ask yourself these questions:

- What is the writer's main claim or question?
- If you cannot find a specific claim, what is the writer's main focus?
- What are the key ideas or concepts that the writer discusses?
- What are the key terms? How does the writer define those terms?

Respond

As you read, write down your thoughts. Ask these questions:

- To what points made by the writer should I respond?
- What ideas might be developed or interpreted differently?
- What do I need to look up?

Analyze

On your second reading, analyze the structure by asking the following questions:

- How is the piece of writing organized?
- What does the writer assume the readers know and believe?
- Where is the evidence? Can you think of contradictory evidence?
- Does the writer acknowledge opposing views? Does the writer deal fairly with opposing views?
- What kinds of sources are cited? Are they thoroughly documented?
- How does the writer represent herself or himself?

2b Become a Critical Viewer

Like critical reading, critical viewing requires you to reflect in depth on what you see. Use the three strategies discussed here.

Preview

Critical viewing requires thinking about the context first.

- Who created this image?
- Why was it created?
- Where and when did it first appear?
- What media are used?
- What has been written about the creator or the image?

Respond

Make notes as you view the image with these questions in mind:

- What was my first impression of the image?
- After thinking more—perhaps reading more—about it, how have I changed or expanded my first impression?

Analyze

The following analytical questions apply primarily to still images:

- How is the image composed or framed?
- Where do my eyes go first?
- How does the image appeal to the values of the audience?
- Was it intended to serve a purpose besides art or entertainment?

To analyze the image in Figure 2.1, Charles briefly summarizes the context then connects the image composition with his impressions about its meaning.

I took an image of an oil train and posted it to my Facebook account. Initially, I took the image because I was bored—I had been held up again by another of the increasingly frequent kilometre-long trains shipping oil from Edmonton to the United

Figure 2.1 An oil train outside of Edmonton, Alberta.

States. From my perspective, the trains transporting oil were the direct result of a lack of pipelines to take the oil to markets. Trains were a more expensive and more dangerous method of transporting oil, as the Lac Megantic and other rail accidents involving oil cars had shown. People opposed to pipeline development saw themselves as fighting a worldwide carbon emissions war with the pipelines as a proxy for the larger problem of emissions. Posting this image to Facebook drew a variety of comments that referred to environmental and economic issues.

The image of rail cars shows the black cars in the foreground, these massive cylinders holding something like 130,000 liters of oil in each car. The image recedes into the distance creating a vanishing pointlike perspective, something that contrasts with the natural surroundings. The vanishing point perspective suggests the infinite length of the train and suggests the repeated trips that these trains make, every day, all year long. The tubular shape in some ways suggests the shape of a pipeline, as if the train is itself a kind of pipeline or has some connection to pipelines. The contrast with the natural surroundings—which are not linear, tubular, or black— also suggests the imposition of human will upon nature.

3 | Planning Your Approach

QUICK*TAKE*

- Write a working thesis (see p. 9)
- Organize your ideas (see pp. 10–11)

3a Identify Key Verbs

Assignments often contain key words and verbs such as *analyze, define, describe,* or *evaluate* that will help you determine your purpose and goals.

- **Analyze:** Find connections among a set of facts, events, or readings and make them meaningful.
- **Define:** Make a claim about how something should be characterized.
- **Describe:** Observe carefully and select details that create an image or impression.
- **Evaluate:** Argue that something is good, bad, best, or worst, according to criteria that you specify.
- **Propose:** Describe a particular problem and explain why your solution is best.

Write a Working Thesis

A clear and specific focus sets up the rest of your essay.

Use questions to focus a broad topic

"What are anarchists" is a big topic. Narrow it by posing questions:

- Why were anarchists at the Toronto G-20 meeting in 2010?
- Why does globalization spark protests from anarchists?
- What values and beliefs unite people under the idea of anarchy?

Consider other angles to expand a narrow topic

Sometimes a topic is too narrow. The following topic defines a very specific event—adopting the new flag—and specifies a very specific outcome—European reactions:

> The Pearson government's attempts to build a sense of nationalism in Canada by adopting a new flag succeeded in creating a strong, internationally respected national profile in the United Kingdom.

Consider broadening your topic by not specifying the details about how something was accomplished and by not specifying who is affected by these events.

Turn your topic into a thesis statement

A thesis states the main idea in your paper. Most of the essay writing that you do in post-secondary education will use an explicit thesis, usually stated near the beginning. The thesis should be closely tied to your purpose—to explain an aspect of your topic or to argue for a position.

Topic: national identity

Vague Thesis: National identity is a flawed concept.

Specific Thesis: National identity is a flawed concept that nevertheless works because it allows groups of people to organize themselves and negotiate their differences relatively peacefully.

Specific Thesis: This paper will examine how a specific health indicator—gestational diabetes—influences the health of pregnant women and, after the birth, the health of their babies.

Specific Thesis: Leisure in the Klondike boomtown created and enforced a particular kind of masculinity in contrast to the "rational recreation" of more established cities and towns in the Northwest.

Organize Your Assignment

Working outline

A working outline resembles an initial sketch of how you plan to arrange your major sections. Before you begin writing, write down main points and the important subpoints to serve as a guide as you draft. Check the assignment sheet for guidelines about how to organize your essay.

Formal outline

Begin a formal outline with your thesis statement. Each numbered or lettered item clearly supports the thesis, and the relationship among the items is clear from the outline hierarchy. Roman numerals indicate the highest level; next come capital letters, then Arabic numbers, and finally lowercase letters. The rule to remember when deciding whether you need to use the next level down is that each level must have at least two items: a "1." needs a "2."; an "a." needs a "b." Formal outlines can be helpful because they force you to look carefully at your organization.

Discipline-specific organization

In some of the social sciences and the lab sciences, research reports follow a specific organization, beginning with an abstract that briefly summarizes the whole report, followed by specific sections and a list of references. This pattern of organization allows other researchers to find specific types of information easily and quickly.

Organization for a report using APA style

1. **Abstract:** Brief summary of the key points of the report
2. **Title of paper**

3. **Introduction with thesis statement:** Section appears without a subtitle.
4. **Body:** The text may include specific topic headings such as
   Health indicators
   The Population Health Promotion Model
   Research studies
   PHPM applied to two studies
5. **Conclusion:** Suggestions for further research

Organization for a report in the sciences or engineering

1. **Abstract:** Brief Summary of the key points of the report
2. **Introduction:** Purpose and background of the experiment being reported
3. **Methods and materials:** The lab manual used or the procedures used to conduct the experiment
4. **Procedure:** Description of what was actually done in the experiment
5. **Results:** Report using both text and graphs to discuss the results of the experiment
6. **Discussion:** An analysis of what can be explained from the results
7. **Conclusion:** A statement of what new knowledge the experiment created

Organization for an essay in the humanities

1. **Introduction:** Description of the topic being discussed. Begin with an example to illustrate the problem under discussion or a surprising fact or a fascinating quotation. Interest your readers and inform them of the topic. Include a thesis statement.
2. **Body of the essay:** The primary discussion of the topic. Include transition words and phrases to help readers identify your main points and follow your shifts in argument.
3. **Conclusion:** A summary of what has already been said. Unless your topic is complex and repetition helps readers understand your main points, conclude by proposing a course of action, pondering the larger significance of the topic, or posing an important question for readers to consider.
4. **Headings:** Do not use headings in a humanities essay unless the instructor requires them.

Compose a Draft

Essays typically contain an introduction, body, and conclusion. You do not have to draft these parts in that order, though. You may want to begin with your best example, which might be in the third paragraph according to your informal or working outline. The most important thing about drafting is to get something written. Quality comes from revising, but to revise you need to have a text to work from. Just get started.

 ## Focus Your Paragraphs

Within a paragraph, readers expect sentences to be closely related to one another. When that occurs, paragraphs are *coherent* (they "flow"). When you revise your paragraphs, check for a clear focus (coherence).

Topic sentences

Topic sentences inform readers of the focus of the paragraph and help writers to maintain a focus on one topic. Such sentences should identify the focus of the paragraph and link it to the larger argument and to your thesis. Topic sentences, however, do not have to begin paragraphs, and they need not be just one sentence.

 ## Write Effective Introductory and Concluding Paragraphs

Effective introductory paragraphs convince the reader to continue reading and set the tone for the rest of the assignment.

Three ways to start an introductory paragraph

A Concisely Stated Thesis

If the pine beetle devastates the forest industry in British Columbia, it will cause a recession in Ontario.

Images

Flames shoot hundreds of metres in the air in a spectacular display of power. The charred remains of one family's home sits within metres of homes that are untouched by the same wildfire.

A Problem

Forest management staff fear that the number of mountain pine beetles has reached epidemic proportions—fires, mudslides, and bankruptcies may result from the appetites of millions of these centimetre-long bugs.

Conclude with strength

Concluding paragraphs connect readers with the larger context of what they've just read. Use the ending paragraph to bridge from your key points to their implications. How does your topic relate to your readers' world?

Issue a Call to Action

Although the mountain pine beetle seems like an overwhelming menace, property owners can take steps to minimize its effects on their lands.

Make Recommendations

Silviculturalists urge property owners to use spacing strategies to limit the damage mountain pine beetles can cause. Spacing allows wind to disperse concentrations of beetles, encourages strong trees that are less susceptible to attacks, and makes it easier for predators to destroy the beetles.

Speculate About the Future

The measures that forestry experts have developed in the early stages of this epidemic may enable us to limit the devastation the beetle can cause.

3g **Link Paragraphs Together**

Write transitions between paragraphs to help your reader follow your argument. Use transition terms to signal relationships between your paragraphs.

Transition terms

- **To contrast:** *although, but, even though, however, in contrast, conversely, in spite of, instead, nevertheless, nonetheless, on the one hand, on the contrary, on the other hand, still, though, yet*
- **To compare:** *again, also, in the same way, likewise, similarly*
- **To signal cause or effect:** *as a result, because, consequently, for this reason, hence, if, so, then, therefore, thus*
- **To conclude:** *as a result, hence, in conclusion, in short, on the whole, therefore, thus*

 # Writing Arguments

QuickTAKE

- Find an arguable topic (see p. 15)
- Organize your position argument (see pp. 16–18)

 4a **Write Position Arguments and Proposal Arguments**

How you develop a written argument depends on your goals. You may want to convince your readers to change their way of thinking about an issue or perhaps get them to consider the issue from your perspective. Or you may want your readers to take some course of action based on your argument. These two kinds of arguments can be characterized as **position arguments** and **proposal arguments**.

4b Find an Arguable Topic and Make a Claim

Position arguments often take two forms: definition arguments and rebuttal arguments.

Definition arguments. People argue about definitions (for example, is graffiti vandalism or is it art?) because of the consequences of something being defined in a certain way. If you can get your audience to accept your definition, then your argument will usually be successful.

Definition arguments take the form shown here:

> Something is (or is not) _____ because it has (or does not have) Criterion A, Criterion B, and Criterion C.

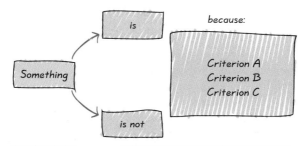

Graffiti is art because it is a means of self-expression, it shows an understanding of design principles, and it stimulates both the senses and the mind.

Rebuttal Arguments. You can take the opposite position and challenge the criteria a writer uses to make a definition or you can challenge the evidence that supports the claim. Often the evidence presented is incomplete or wrong. Sometimes you can find counterevidence. When you rebut an argument, you often identify one or more fallacies in that argument.

Rebuttal arguments take this form:

> The opposing argument has serious shortcomings that undermine the claim because
>
>   flawed reason 1
>
>   flawed reason 2

because:

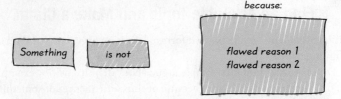

Something | is not | flawed reason 1
flawed reason 2

The great white shark gained a false reputation as a "man eater" from the 1975 movie *Jaws*, but in fact attacks on humans are rare and most bites have been "test bites," which is a common shark behavior with unfamiliar objects.

Supporting claims with reasons

The difference between a slogan, such as *Oppose candidate X*, and an arguable claim, such as *Oppose candidate X because she will not lower taxes and not improve schools*, is the presence of a reason linked to the claim. A reason is typically offered in a ***because clause***, a statement that begins with the word *because* and provides a supporting reason for the claim. The word *because* signals a **link** between the reason and the claim.

 4c **Organize and Write a Position Argument**

1 Think before you write

Focus on your readers
- What do your readers already know about the subject?
- What is their attitude toward the subject? If it is different from your position, how can you address the difference?
- What are the chances of changing the opinions and beliefs of your readers? If your readers are unlikely to be moved, can you get them to acknowledge that your position is reasonable?
- Are there any sensitive issues you should be aware of?

2 | Write an introduction

Engage your readers quickly
- Get your readers' attention with an example of what is at stake.
- Define the subject or issue.
- State your thesis to announce your position.

3 | Organize and write the body of your paper

Develop reasons
- Can you argue from a definition? Is ____ a ____?
  Are cheerleaders athletes?
  Are zoos guilty of cruelty to animals?
- Can you compare and contrast? Is ____ like or unlike ____?
- Can you argue that something is good (better, bad, worse)?
- Can you argue that something caused (or may cause) something else?
- Can you refute objections to your position?

Support reasons with evidence
- Can you support your reasons by going to a site and making observations?
- Can you find facts, statistics, or statements from authorities to support your reasons?

Consider opposing views
- Acknowledge other stakeholders for the issue, and consider their positions.
- Explain why your position is preferable.
- Make counterarguments if necessary.

4 | Write a conclusion

End with more than a summary
- Offer further evidence in support of your thesis.
- Reinforce what is at stake.
- Give an example that gets at the heart of the issue.

Revise, revise, revise

Evaluate your draft
- Make sure your position argument meets the assignment requirements.
- Can you sharpen your thesis to make your position clearer?
- Can you add additional reasons to strengthen your argument?
- Can you supply additional evidence?
- When you have finished revising, edit and proofread carefully.

5 Writing in Academic Genres

QUICK*TAKE*

- Identify the genre your instructor wants (throughout)
- Organize your document based on its genre (throughout)
- Prepare your information to fit the genre format (throughout)

 ## Write an Observation

Observations are common in the natural sciences and in social science disciplines such as psychology, sociology, and education. While they differ slightly from discipline to discipline, observations generally require you (the researcher) to examine visually and describe in detail the appearance or behaviour of some kind of object, individual, or phenomenon. When you take notes for an observation, include as many relevant and specific details as appropriate.

Elements of an observation

Precise title	Aim to communicate your topic clearly and concisely.
Context	Be specific about what or whom you are observing. How did you limit your site or subject? What background information do readers need?
Record of observations	Report what you observed in some logical order: chronologically, from most obvious features to least obvious, or some other pattern.
Conclusion or summary	Give your readers a framework in which to understand your observations. What conclusions can you draw from them? What questions are left unanswered?

What you need to do

- Carry a notebook and make extensive field notes. Provide as much information as possible about the activities you observe.
- Record in your notebook exactly when you arrived and left, where you were, and exactly what you saw and heard.
- Analyze your observations before you write about them. Identify patterns, and organize your report according to those patterns.

Sample observation

Part A: The effect of selected antibiotics on microbial growth
Antibiotic discs were placed on Mueller-Hinton agar that
had been streaked with the specific micro-organism and
then incubated for 24 hours. The different zones that
were observed are listed in the table below.

Table 1. *Zones of Clearing of Various Antibiotics on
Microbial Growth When Grown on Mueller-Hinton Agar*

	Escherichia coli-63	Escherichia coli-BG	Staphylococcus aureus	Candida albicans
Penicillin	—	—	39 mm	23 mm
Tetracycline	26 mm	10.5 mm	30 mm	—
Polymyxin-B	16 mm	15.5 mm	—	9 mm
Erythromycin	—	11 mm	28 mm	—
Cyclohexamide	—	9 mm	24 mm	32 mm
Ampicillin	20 mm	—	31.5 mm	8 mm (patchy)

Specific terms, sizes, and descriptive phrases used

When compared to the interpretive chart, the strain
of S. aureus used in this lab behaved according to
the expected results for each antibiotic except for
polymyxin-B (7). The expected zone of clearing is
between 7 and 13 mm, but none was observed on the
plate. A zone of clearing of that size is quite small,
and it is possible that it was missed. Because all of
the other results for S. aureus are within the expected
range, the results should still be valid.

5b Write a Scholarly Essay in the Humanities

Instructors use a wide variety of terms to describe the kind of essay or paper that focuses on research: research essay, scholarly essay, major essay, term paper. To produce the kind of essay the instructor wants to read, obtain answers to the questions in the table below.

Question	Action
What verbs do instructors use to describe your purpose in the assignment?	Possible answers: *analyze/historically analyze; describe; compare; explore* (see Chapter 4).
Does the verb suggest how to organize your essay?	Possible answer: "compare" suggests a comparison/contrast paper.
Do instructors require sources? If so, do they specify what kinds of sources?	Use database searches; click on "peer reviewed" in the search box. See Part 2 for more details.
Do they use the word "scholarly," "research," or "critically" in the description of the assignment?	Identify what sources you should use—for example, readings from class textbooks—to establish a theory or model you can apply to the specific topic of the essay.
Do they provide a rubric or scoring guide they will use to mark the essays?	If they do, read it carefully to identify criteria they will look for when they grade: kinds of sources, citation styles; thesis statements.
Do they specify an audience for the assignment? If not, what do you know about your instructor as a reader?	Will your instructor find this topic interesting? Might you revise your approach to make the topic more interesting? Will your reflections on the topic be of interest to your instructor?

Organizational pattern for an essay in the humanities

Introduction	Consider using an example, surprising fact, or fascinating quotation to begin. Identify the topic and include a thesis statement somewhere in the introduction.

EXAMPLE

Free enterprise capitalism in the Klondike contributed to a dominant ideological stance that valued the free choice of individuals to pursue whatever leisure activities they wanted—including gambling, drinking to excess, and womanizing—with few, if any, restraints.

Body	Consider listing the parts of the topic of your paper in your thesis statement; in the body of the essay, follow the order you used in the thesis statement. Do not use headings unless your instructor requires them.
	EXAMPLE
	Gambling
	Drinking to excess
	Womanizing
	Use topic sentences and transitions to guide your reader as you change topics from one paragraph to another.
Conclusion	Summarize your argument. Consider proposing a course of action that follows from the argument in the essay. Consider widening the scope of your essay to suggest the implications of your argument—how does it connect to the bigger picture?

5c Write a Scholarly Essay in Nursing

Scholarly essays in nursing differ from the humanities in structure—they follow the APA style for the headings—and in the way they argue. Nursing essays often require students to summarize research and reflect on implications of that research for their practices as nurses.

Elements of a scholarly essay in nursing

Abstract	Summarizes the key points of the report
Title of paper	Includes a precise title
Introduction with thesis statement—no subtitle for this section	Identifies the topic and your argument

Body	The text may include these topics:
	   Health indicators
	   The Population Health Promotion Model
	     (PHPM)
	   Research studies
	   PHPM applied

Conclusion	Suggestions for further research

5d Write an Engineering Report

Reports in engineering courses focus less on arguing a position and more on summarizing and evaluating information. Instructors ask students to identify implications and applications of technologies when writing reports. Information reports in the sciences or engineering fields often use headings that examine the different aspects of a technology.

Elements of a report in engineering

Abstract	Summarizes the key points of the report
Table of contents	Lists the headings in the report
Body	The body will be organized around headings drawn from the topic you choose, as in this example: 1. History of computers in medicine 2. Applications of the technology 3. Advantages/disadvantages 4. Implications for society 5. Possible future applications
Conclusion	Suggests further research

5e Write a Lab Report

Lab reports follow a strict structure, enabling specialists in a given field to assess quickly the experimental methods and findings in any report. Check with your instructor for the specific elements required for your lab report.

Elements of a lab report

Title	State exactly what was tested, using language specific to the field.
Abstract	Briefly state the questions and the findings in the report.
Introduction	Give the full context of the problem, defining the hypothesis being tested.

Methods	Describe the materials used as well as the method of investigation. Your methods and procedure sections should be specific enough to allow another researcher to replicate your experiment.
Procedure	Step by step, narrate exactly what you did and what happened. In most fields, you will use the passive voice.
Results	State the outcomes you obtained, providing carefully labelled charts and graphics as needed.
Discussion	State why you think you got the results you did, using your results to explain. If there were anomalies in your data, note them as well.
Conclusion	Briefly explain what was learned from this experiment. What still needs to be investigated?
References	Using the appropriate format, cite all the outside sources you have used. (See Chapter 15 for pyschology lab reports and Chapter 17 for science lab reports.)

What you need to do

- Understand the question you are researching and the process you will use before you begin. Ask your instructor when you need clarification.
- Take thorough notes at each step of your process. You may be asked to keep a lab notebook with a specific format for recording data. Review your notes before you begin drafting your report.
- Don't get ahead of yourself. Keep methods, procedure, discussion, and conclusion sections separate. Remember that other scientists will look at specific sections of your report expecting to find certain kinds of information. If that information isn't where they expect it to be, your report will not make sense.
- Write your abstract last. Writing all the other sections of the report first will give you a much clearer picture of your findings.

5f   Write an Essay Exam

Instructors use essay exams to test your understanding of course concepts and to assess your ability to analyze ideas independently. To demonstrate these skills, you must write an essay that responds directly and fully to the question being asked.

Elements of an exam essay

Introduction	Briefly restate the question, summarizing the answer you will provide.
Body paragraphs	Each paragraph should address a major element of the question. Order paragraphs so the reader can tell how you are responding to the question.
	EXAMPLE
	Of the many factors leading to the downfall of Brian Mulroney's government, implementing the GST was the most important.
Conclusion	*Briefly* restate your answer to the question, not the question itself.

What you need to do

- Make sure you understand the question. Respond with the kinds of information and analysis the question asks you to provide.
- Plan your response before you begin writing, using an outline, list, or diagram. Note how much time you have to write your response.
- Address each element of the question, providing supporting evidence.
- Relate the point of each paragraph clearly to the larger argument.
- Save a few minutes to proofread and add information where needed.

6 | Writing in Online and Multimedia Genres

QUICK*TAKE*

- Learn how to compose a blog or a discussion post (see below)
- Learn how to create a multimedia project (see p. 27)

6a Compose Blogs and Discussion Posts

Blogs assigned for courses sometimes allow students a great deal of freedom to select their subject matter; sometimes course blogs are on an assigned topic, such as responses to the readings. Discussion board posts are often similar to blogs, but they are typically written as a response to a question or posting by the instructor.

Elements of a successful blog

Title	Include an informative title.
Content	Offer something new. If you don't have anything new, then point readers to the interesting writing of others.
Writing style	Engage readers with a conversational style.
Reader friendliness	Revise your entry to make it more readable and to catch errors.
Participation	Invite responses.

What you need to do

- Develop a personal voice that conveys your personality.
- Remember that your blog is a conversation. You want to get responses to what you write.
- Do your homework. Let your readers know the sources of your information.
- Keep it short. If you have a lot to say about different subjects, write more than one entry.

- Add images if they are needed.
- Provide relevant links.
- Remember that informal writing is not sloppy, error-filled writing.

6b Create Multimedia Projects

If you decide to create a multimedia project, find out what resources are available for students on your campus. Many post-secondary institutions have digital media labs, which offer workshops and can provide video and audio studios, technical assistance, equipment, and software.

Oral presentation with visuals

- **Example project:** *Address to local town meeting about establishing more no-kill animal shelters in your city*
- **Plan:** Visit animal shelters, interview volunteers, and take photographs. Then determine the key points you want to make.
- **Produce:** Use simple design for your slides and avoid putting much text on them. Use your own quality photographs and simple charts and graphs to emphasize the main points.
- **Deliver:** Practice in advance, and pay attention to the timing of your slides. Involve your audience by inviting responses. Finish on time or earlier.

Essay with images

- **Example project:** *Evaluation argument concerning the poor condition of parks in your city*
- **Plan:** Visit several parks, make notes, and take photographs.
- **Produce:** Write an essay. Edit your images with an image editor and insert them in your essay with captions.
- **Edit:** Revise with the comments of classmates and your instructor.

Sample blog entry

BLOG | **Posted by Jillian Akbar at 4:18 p.m. October 5, 2014**
3 comments

Sara Macdonald's *Holy Cow* (2002)

Sara Macdonald does not begin her voyage from Australia to India with the happiest of outlooks. Laden with memories of the terrible time she had there eleven years earlier, at first she finds her only consolation in being with her boyfriend Jonathan, a fellow journalist. Macdonald confesses that her motives are more than just companionship:

> Leaving my wonderful job was the hardest thing I've ever done but perhaps I didn't do it just for love. A part of me wanted to reclaim myself, to redefine my identity, to grow up professionally, to embrace anonymity and get rid of the stalker. (17)

Macdonald's account is engaging in her insightful depiction of India. Her observations of cultural norms, such as honoring one's family in marriage, are distant but detailed and nonjudgmental. The chapter titles suggest the irreverent tone and humor of the book, including "Sex, Lies and Saving Face," "Three Weddings and a Funeral," "Insane in the Membrane," "Birds of a Feather Become Extinct Together," and "Hail Mary and Good-bye God."

Macdonald's attitude toward India lightens up in the second half of the book, and I finally could relate as she suffered an Indian summer with nothing but a television and power cuts—exactly like my boyfriend's apartment in August. She offers more on the exotic imagery of India: a lotus flower growing out of slimy water, a pink ten-foot high Mary in a sari, and the "candy-colored kingdom" of the Divine Mother in Kerala (199). She includes my favorite image of all when she returns to India and is submerged in "India's Kaleidoscipe of Technicolor" to feel "like Dorothy in the land of Oz" (276).

Audio production

- **Example project:** *Oral history of neighborhood residents making a causal argument about why a neighborhood declined after a freeway was built through the middle of it*
- **Plan:** Arrange and record interviews and write a script.
- **Produce:** Reserve a campus audio production lab or record on your computer. Create an audio file by combining the interviews with your narration. Export the video into a format such as WAV or MP3 that you can put on the web or share as a downloadable file.
- **Edit:** Edit with an audio editor.

Video production

- **Example project:** *Proposal to create bike lanes on a busy street near your campus*
- **Plan:** Identify locations, get permission to film if necessary, and write a script.
- **Produce:** Shoot video of the street with cars and bikes competing. Interview cyclists, drivers, and local business owners about their sense of urgency of the problem and the effects of creating bike lanes.
- **Edit:** Edit with a video editor. Export the video into a format such as QuickTime that you can put on the web or share as a downloadable file.

7 | Revising, Editing, and Proofreading

QUICK*TAKE*

- Use strategies for rewriting (see below)
- Edit for specific goals (see p. 31)

7a Evaluate Your Draft

Use the following questions to evaluate your draft. Note any places where you might make improvements.

- Does your paper or project meet the requirements of the assignment?
- Does your writing have a clear focus?
- Are your main points adequately developed?
- Is your organization effective?
- Do you consider your readers' knowledge and points of view?
- Do you represent yourself effectively?
- Do you conclude emphatically?

When you finish, make a list of your goals for the revision.

7b Learn Strategies for Rewriting

1. **Keep your audience in mind.** Reread each paragraph's opening sentence. Is the language strong and engaging enough to keep your reader interested?
2. **Sharpen your focus wherever possible.** Revise your thesis and supporting paragraphs so that your reader sees the connection between them.
3. **Check that key terms are adequately defined.** What are your key terms? Are they defined precisely enough to be meaningful?
4. **Develop ideas where necessary.** Identify short paragraphs: key points and claims may need more explanation and supporting evidence.

5. **Check links between paragraphs.** Underline the first and last sentences of each paragraph in your paper and then read these underlined sentences aloud to a friend. Do these sentences together make a logical and coherent argument?
6. **Consider your title.** Be as specific as you can in your title, and, if possible, suggest your stance.
7. **Consider your introduction.** In the introduction you want to get off to a fast start and convince your reader to keep reading.
8. **Consider your conclusion.** Try to leave your reader with something interesting and provocative.

7c Edit for Specific Goals

1. **Check the connections between sentences.** If you need to signal the relationship from one sentence to the next, use a transitional word or phrase.
2. **Check your sentences.** If you notice that a sentence is hard to read or doesn't sound right when you read your paper aloud, rephrase it.
3. **Eliminate wordiness.** See how many words you can take out without losing the meaning (see pp. 180–185).
4. **Use active verbs.** Any time you can use a verb other than a form of *be* (*is, are, was, were*) and a verb ending in *ing*, take advantage of the opportunity to make your style more lively.
5. **Use specific and inclusive language.** As you read, stay alert for any vague words or phrases. Check to make sure that you have used inclusive language throughout (see pp. 195–197).

7d Proofread Carefully

1. **Know what your spell-checker can and cannot do.** Spell-checkers do not catch wrong words (e.g., "to much" should be "too much"), missing endings ("three dog"), and other, similar errors.
2. **Check for grammar and mechanics.** Nothing hurts your credibility with readers more than a text with numerous errors.

7e Review the Writing of Others

Your instructor may ask you to review your classmates' drafts.

1. **Begin with the big picture.** Ask the questions in Section 7a about whether the project meets the assignment, and so on.
2. **Call attention to local problems last.** Review sentence construction, word choice, and errors at a later point.
3. **Write a note to the writer.** Include a summary of your comments.

8 | Designing and Presenting

QUICKTAKE

- Design visually coherent presentation materials (see below)
- Determine how best to shape your presentation (see p. 34)

8a Learn Design Basics

Consider your page layout:

1. What are the main elements of the design?
2. Which element(s) is/are most important?

The basic principles of good design

- Create visual relationships among elements on the page.
- Make similar items look similar.
- Make different items look different.

The Writing Process: A Model

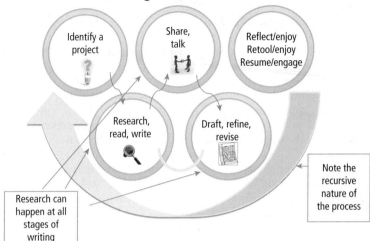

Figure 8.1   The design of this presentation slide directs reader/viewer attention to certain elements and creates a professional impression.

Figure 8.1 uses callout boxes and arrows to direct reader/viewer attention to explanatory points about the visual. Size visually distinguishes the title of the slide from the details. Centred alignment of the text throughout visually organizes the information presented in the slide.

8b Present Effectively

New technologies make it easy to produce high-quality visuals to accompany oral presentations (see Figure 8.1), but these technologies also offer many choices that place new demands on speakers. The key to success is remembering that your purpose is to communicate effectively. In any medium, your goals, your subject, and your audience should shape your presentation.

Basics for effective presentations

- **Analyze your task:** What *kind* of presentation are you giving? Informative, how-to, persuasive, summary, or group presentation?
- **Think about where you will give your presentation:** Find out if the room has limitations (acoustic, lighting, technology) and plan to overcome them.
- **Select your topic:** Choose a topic that interests you and your audience.
- **Think about the scope of your topic:** How long is your presentation? Suit the scope of your topic to the time you have available to speak.
- **Consider your audience:** Assess how your audience will respond to your topic. Should you include background so they will understand?
- **Organize your presentation:** Choose from among chronological, topical, and problem/solution methods.
- **Support your presentation:** Include evidence to support the claims in your talk.
- **Include relevant visuals:** Decide which ones are most appropriate— outline, text, statistical charts, flowcharts, photographs, models, maps.
- **Plan your introduction:** Use the first two minutes to get your audience's attention and give them an overview of your subject and why it's important.
- **Plan your conclusion:** End on a strong note by using an example or idea that captures the main point of your speech that listeners will remember.

8c Deliver a Presentation With Visuals

Visuals make an important contribution to any presentation. They can highlight your important points for audience members. You can also maintain your audience's attention by giving them relevant and interesting visuals to look at. Finally, use visuals to help you make a complex discussion more easily understood.

Nervousness

Nervousness is usually invisible. If you make a mistake, remember that your audience will understand. Stage fright is normal, and often you can draw off that energy to make a more forceful presentation. Take a deep breath before you begin, and smile.

Practice

There is no substitute for rehearsing your speech several times.

- You will become more confident.
- You will be able to focus more on your audience and on maintaining eye contact.
- You will be more comfortable using your visuals.
- You will know how long your presentation will take.

Effective techniques

- Practise in advance.
- Believe in what you say; enthusiasm is contagious.
- Talk, don't read.
- Stand, don't sit.
- Make eye contact.
- Signal main points with gestures.
- Speak loudly.
- Use effective visuals.
- Focus on main points.
- Give an overview in the introduction.
- Give a conclusion that ends with a key idea or example.
- Finish on time.

PART 2

Planning Research and Finding Sources

RESEARCH MAP: CONDUCTING RESEARCH

College research writing requires that you

- determine your goals,
- find a topic,
- ask a question about that topic,
- find out what has been written about that topic,
- evaluate what has been written about that topic, and
- make a contribution to the discussion about that topic.

There are four key steps in planning research and finding sources.

1 | Plan the research project

To analyze what you are being asked to do, go to Section 9a.

To ask a question about a topic that interests you and to narrow that topic, go to 9b.

To determine what kinds of research you will need, go to 9d.

Conduct field research if it is appropriate for your project. To see strategies for

- **Conducting Interviews**, go to 12b.
- **Administering Surveys**, go to 12c.
- **Making Observations**, go to 12d.

2 | Draft a working thesis

To draft a working thesis, go to 9c.

To create a working bibliography, go to 9e.

3 | Find and track sources

Consult with a research librarian if possible, and determine where and how to start looking.

- To find sources in **Databases**, go to 10e.
- To find sources on the **Web**, go to 10f.
- To find **Print** sources, go to 10c.
- To keep track of sources, go to 10d.

4 | Evaluate sources

Decide which sources are going to be useful for your project:

- To determine the **Relevance** of each source to your research question, go to 11a.

Evaluate the different types of sources you are using:

- For **Database** and **Print** sources, go to 11b.
- For **Web** sources, go to 11d.

9 | Planning Your Research

QUICKTAKE

- Analyze the assignment (see below)
- Find and narrow a topic (see p. 41)
- Draft a working thesis (see p. 43)

9a Analyze the Research Task

If you have an assignment that requires research, look closely at what you are being asked to do.

Determine your purpose

- An *analysis* or *examination* requires you to look at an issue in detail, explaining how it has evolved, who or what it affects, and what is at stake.
- A *review of scholarship* requires you to summarize what key scholars and researchers have written about the issue.
- An *evaluation* requires you to make critical judgments.
- An *argument* requires you to assemble evidence in support of a claim you make.

Identify your potential readers

- How familiar are your readers with your subject?
- What background information will you need to supply?
- If your subject is controversial, what opinions or beliefs are your readers likely to hold?

Assess the project's length, scope, and requirements

- What kind of research are you being asked to do?
- What is the length of the project?

- What kinds and number of sources or field research are required?
- Which documentation style—such as MLA (see Chapter 14) or APA (see Chapter 15)—is required?

9b Find and Narrow a Topic

You might begin by doing one or more of the following:

- **Visit a category such as "Research by Subject" on your library's website.** Clicking on a subject such as "African and African American Studies" will take you to a list of online resources. Often you can find an e-mail link to a reference librarian who can assist you.
- **Look for topics in your courses.** Browse your course notes and readings. Are there any topics you might want to explore in greater depth?
- **Consult a specialized encyclopedia.** Specialized encyclopedias focus on a single area of knowledge, go into more depth about a subject, and often include bibliographies. Check if your library database page has a link to the Gale Virtual Reference Library, which offers entries from many specialized encyclopedias and reference sources.
- **Look for topics as you read.** When you read actively, you ask questions and respond to ideas in the text. Review what you wrote in the margins or the notes you have made about something you read that interested you. You may find a potential topic.

It can be tricky to find a balance between what you want to say about a topic and the amount of space you have to say it in. Usually your instructor will suggest a length for your project, which should help you decide how to limit your topic. If you suspect your topic is becoming unmanageable and your project may be too long, look for ways to narrow your focus.

Off track	A 5-page paper on European witch hunts
On track	A 5-page paper tracing two or three major causes of the European witch hunts of the fifteenth and sixteenth centuries
Off track	A 10-page paper on accounting fraud
On track	A 10-page paper examining how a new law would help prevent corporate accounting fraud

Ask questions about your topic

When you have a topic that is interesting to you, manageable in scope, and possible to research using sources or doing field research, then your next task is to ask researchable questions.

Explore a definition

- While many (most) people think X is a Y, can X be better thought of as a Z?

  Most people think of deer as harmless animals that are benign to the environment, but their overpopulation devastates young trees in forests, leading to loss of habitat for birds and other species that depend on those trees.

Evaluate a person, activity, or thing

- Can you argue that a person, activity, or thing is either good, better, or best (or bad, worse, or worst) within its class?

  Fender Stratocasters from the 1950s remain the best electric guitars ever made because of their versatility, sound quality, and player-friendly features.

Examine why something happened

- Can you argue that while there were obvious causes of Y, Y would not have occurred had it not been for X?

  Students are called irresponsible when they run up high credit card debts that they cannot pay off, but these debts would not have occurred if credit card companies had not aggressively marketed cards and offered high lines of credit to students with no income.

- Can you argue for an alternative cause rather than the one many people assume?

  While many opponents of the Keystone XL pipeline argue that it would contribute significantly to global warming, they remain silent on what is the largest greenhouse gas source: coal-fired sources.

Counter objections to a position

- Can the reverse or opposite of an opposing claim be argued?

  New medications that relieve pain are welcomed by runners and other athletes, but these drugs also mask signals that our bodies send us, increasing the risk of serious injury.

Propose a solution to a problem

- Can you propose a solution to a local problem?

  The traffic congestion on our campus could be eased by creating bike lanes on University Drive, which would encourage more students, faculty, and staff to commute by bicycle.

9c Draft a Working Thesis

If you ask a focused and interesting research question, your answer will be your **working thesis**. This working thesis will be the focus of the remainder of your research and ultimately your research project.

Topic	Economic impacts of casino gambling
Research Question	How does the presence of a casino affect the economy of the community where it is located?
Working Thesis	The economic impact of casino gambling on the community in which it is located is mixed, with some businesses benefiting and others suffering.

9d Determine What Kind of Research You Need

When you begin your research, you will have to make a few educated guesses about where to look. Ask these questions before you start:

- How much information do you need? The assignment may specify the number of sources you should consult.
- Are particular types of sources required? If so, do you understand why those sources are required?

- How current should the information be? Some assignments require you to use the most up-to-date information you can locate.

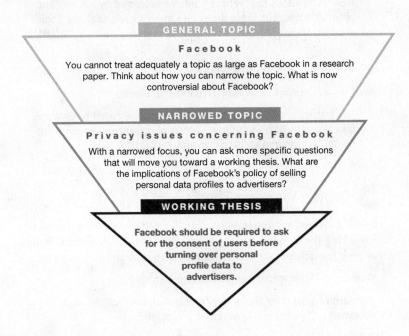

GENERAL TOPIC

Facebook

You cannot treat adequately a topic as large as Facebook in a research paper. Think about how you can narrow the topic. What is now controversial about Facebook?

NARROWED TOPIC

Privacy issues concerning Facebook

With a narrowed focus, you can ask more specific questions that will move you toward a working thesis. What are the implications of Facebook's policy of selling personal data profiles to advertisers?

WORKING THESIS

Facebook should be required to ask for the consent of users before turning over personal profile data to advertisers.

Secondary research

Most people who do research rely partly or exclusively on the work of others as sources of information. Research based on the work of others is called **secondary research**. Chapters 10 and 11 explain in detail how to find and evaluate database, web, and print sources.

Primary research

Much of the research done at a university creates new information through **primary research:** experiments, data-gathering surveys and interviews, detailed observations, and the examination of historical documents. Chapter 12 explains how to plan and conduct three types of field research: interviews (12b), surveys (12c), and observations (12d).

9e Create a Working Bibliography

When you begin to collect your sources, make sure you get full bibliographic information for everything you might want to use in your project: articles, books, websites, and other materials. Decide which documentation style you will use. If your instructor does not tell you which style is appropriate, ask. (The major documentation styles—MLA, APA, CMS, CSE, and IEEE—are dealt with in detail in Chapters 14–18.)

Find the necessary bibliographic information

Chapter 10 gives instructions on what information you will need to collect for each kind of source. In general, as you research and develop a working bibliography, the rule of thumb is to write down more information rather than less. You can always delete unnecessary information when it comes time to format your citations according to your chosen documentation style (APA, MLA, CMS, CSE, or IEEE), but it is time-consuming to go back to sources to find missing bibliographic information.

10 | Finding Sources

QUICKTAKE

- Keep track of sources (see p. 49)
- Find sources in databases (see p. 53)
- Find sources on the web (see p. 53)

10a Develop Strategies for Finding Sources

Libraries still contain many resources not available on the web. Even more important, libraries have professional research librarians who can help you locate sources quickly.

Find the right kinds of sources

Type of source	Type of information	How to find sources
Scholarly books	Extensive and in-depth coverage of nearly any subject	Library catalogue
Scholarly journals	Reports of new knowledge and research findings by experts	Online library databases
Trade journals	Reports of information pertaining to specific industries, professions, and products	Online library databases
Popular magazines	Reports or summaries of current news, sports, fashion, entertainment subjects	Online library databases
Newspapers	Recent and current information: foreign newspapers are useful for international perspectives	Online library databases
Government publications	Government-collected statistics, studies, and reports: especially good for science and medicine	Library catalogue and city, state, and federal government websites
Videos, audios, documentaries, maps	Information varies widely	Library catalogue, web, and online library databases

10b Identify Keywords

Keyword searches allow you to search all fields in the library's catalogue.
Furthermore, keyword searches are the primary way to find information in
library databases (see Section 10e) and on the web (see Section 10f).

Begin with your research question and working thesis.

Topic	Religious symbols in public high schools
Research Question	Does it endanger other students to allow Sikh students to wear ceremonial daggers to school?
Working Thesis	While *traditional weaponry* is *properly banned from Canadian high schools* due to possible *violence,* the ceremonial *dagger worn by Sikh* students poses no threat and should be an *exception* to the ban.

Italicize (as above) the key terms in your thesis. Then think of as many
synonyms and related terms as you can and make lists.

Traditional Weaponry	Canadian High Schools and Violence	Banned Items	Exceptions
daggers worn by Sikhs	violent incidents at secondary schools	cell phones	head coverings (scarves, hats, etc.)
knives	stabbings at secondary schools	pagers	ceremonial weapons
guns	beatings at secondary schools	concealed weapons	kirpans
ceremonial weapons	shootings at high schools	gang wear	wristbands
religious weapons	bullying at secondary schools	inappropriate slogans, logos	ceremonial daggers
arms	harassment at high schools		dirks
	kirpan violence		legal restrictions
	legal discussion of kirpans in schools		

Know the limitations of *Wikipedia*

Wikipedia is a valuable resource for current information and for popular culture topics that are not covered in traditional encyclopedias. You can find out, for example, that SpongeBob SquarePants's original name was "SpongeBoy," but it had already been copyrighted.

Nevertheless, many instructors and the scholarly community in general do not consider *Wikipedia* a reliable source of information for a research project. The fundamental problem with *Wikipedia* is stability, not whether the information is correct or incorrect. *Wikipedia* and other wikis constantly change. The underlying idea of documenting sources is that readers can consult the same sources that you consulted. To be on the safe side, treat *Wikipedia* as you would a blog: Consult other sources to confirm what you find on *Wikipedia*, and cite those sources.

10c Find Print Sources

No matter how current the topic you are researching, you will likely find information in print sources that is simply not available online. Print sources have other advantages as well.

- Books are shelved in libraries according to subject, allowing easy browsing.
- Books often have bibliographies, directing you to other research on the subject.
- You can search for books in multiple ways: author, title, subject, or call letter.
- The majority of print sources have been evaluated by scholars, editors, and publishers, who decided whether they merited publication.

Find books

The floors of your library where books are shelved are referred to as the *stacks*. The call number will enable you to find the item in the stacks. You will need to consult the locations guide for your library, which gives the level and section where an item is shelved.

Find journal articles

Like books, scholarly journals provide in-depth examinations of subjects. The articles in scholarly journals are written by experts, and they usually contain lists of references that can guide you to other research on a subject.

Some instructors frown on using popular magazines, but these publications can be valuable for researching current opinion on a particular topic. Databases increasingly contain the full text of articles, allowing you to read and copy the contents onto your computer.

10d Keep Track of Sources

As you begin to collect your sources, make sure you get full bibliographic information for everything you might want to use in your project. Decide which documentation style you will use. (The major documentation styles—MLA, APA, CMS, CSE, and IEEE—are dealt with in detail in Chapters 14–18.)

Locate elements of a citation in database sources

For any source you find on a database, MLA style requires you to provide the full print information, the name of the database in italics, the medium of publication (*Web*), and the date you accessed the database. If page numbers are not included, use *n. pag.* Do *not* include the URL of the database.

Author's name	Lai, Jodi
Title of article	"Playing the Business Game: Gamification Can Put Fun into Training Programs"
Publication information	
Name of periodical	*Edmonton Journal*
Date of publication (and edition for newspapers)	11 Sept. 2012
Section and page number	B6
Database information	
Name of database	*ProQuest*
Date you accessed the site	27 Mar. 2014

The citation would appear as follows in an MLA-style works-cited list (see Section 14f).

> Lai, Jodi. "Playing the Business Game: Gamification Can Put Fun into Training Programs." *Edmonton Journal* 11 Sept. 2012: B6. *ProQuest*. Web. 27 Mar. 2014.

APA style no longer requires listing the names of common databases or listing the date of access, unless the content is likely to change (see Section 15d). If you name the database, do not list the URL.

> Lai, J. (2012, September 11). Playing the business game: Gamification can put fun into training programs. *Edmonton Journal*, p. B6. Available from *Proquest*.

Locate elements of a citation in web sources

As you conduct your online research, make sure you collect the necessary bibliographic information for everything you might want to use as a source. Because of the potential volatility of web sources (they can and do disappear overnight), their citations require extra information. Depending on the citation format you use, you'll arrange this information in different ways.

Collect the following information about a website:

Author's name, if available (if not, use the associated institution or organization)	Macdonald, June
Title of article	"Gamification 2013: A Conversation with Neil Randall"
Publication information	
Name of site or online journal	*Gamification 2013*
Publisher or sponsor of the site (for MLA style)	University of Waterloo
Date of publication (for an article) or of site's last update	25 Sept. 2013
Date you accessed the site	27 Mar. 2014
URL (for some APA formats including blogs)	https://uwaterloo.ca/gamification/

An MLA works-cited entry for this article would look like this:

> Macdonald, June. "Gamification 2013: A Conversation with Neil Randall." *Gamification 2013*. U of Waterloo, 25 Sept. 2013. Web. 27 Mar. 2014.

In an APA references list, the citation would look like this:

> Macdonald, J. (2013, September 25). Gamification 2013: A conversation with Neil Randall. Article posted to https://uwaterloo.ca/gamification/

Locate elements of a citation in print sources

For books you will need, at minimum, the following information, which can typically be found on the front and back of the title page.

Author's name	Beah, Ishmael
Title of the book	*A Long Way Gone: Memoirs of a boy soldier*
Publication information	
Place of publication	Toronto
Name of publisher	Penguin
Date of publication	2007
Medium of publication	Print

Here's how the book would be cited in an MLA-style works-cited list.

> Beah, Ishmael. *A Long Way Gone: Memoirs of a Boy Soldier*. Toronto: Penguin, 2007. Print.

Here's the APA citation for the same book.

> Beah, I. (2007). *A long way gone: Memoirs of a boy soldier*. Toronto: Penguin.

You will also need the page numbers if you are quoting directly or referring to a specific passage, and the title and author of the individual chapter if your source is an edited book with contributions by several people.

For journals you will need the following:

Author's name	Artemeva, Natasha, and Janna Fox.
Title of article	"Awareness Versus Production: Probing Students' Antecedent Genre Knowledge"
Publication information	
Name of journal	*Journal of Business and Technical Communication*
Volume number and issue number	24.4
Date of publication (and edition for newspapers)	2010
Page numbers of the article	476-515
Medium of publication	Print
Document Object Identifier (DOI), if available, for APA	10.1177/1050651910371302

An entry in an MLA-style works-cited list would look like this:

Artemeva, Natasha, and Janna Fox. "Awareness Versus Production: Probing Students' Antecedent Genre Knowledge." *Journal of Business and Technical Communication* 24.4 (2010): 476-515.

An entry in APA style would look like this:

Artemeva, N., & Fox, J. (2010). Awareness versus production: Probing students' antecedent genre knowledge. *Journal of Business and Technical Communication, 24,* 476-515. doi:10.1177/1050651910371302.

Find Sources in Databases

Common Databases

Academic OneFile	Indexes periodicals from the arts, humanities, sciences, social sciences, and general news, with full-text articles and images.

Academic Search Premier and Complete	Provides full-text articles for thousands of scholarly publications.
ArticleFirst	Indexes journals in business, the humanities, medicine, science, and social sciences.
Business Search Premier and Complete	Provides full-text articles in all business disciplines.
EBSCOhost Research Databases	Provides gateway to a large collection of EBSCO databases, including *Academic Search Premier and Complete, Business Source Premier and Complete, ERIC,* and *Medline.*
Google Books	Allows searches within books and provides snippets surrounding search terms for copyrighted books. Many books out of copyright have the full text. Available for everyone.
Google Scholar	Searches scholarly literature according to criteria of relevance. Available for everyone.
General OneFile	Contains millions of full-text articles about a wide range of academic and general-interest topics.
JSTOR	Provides scanned copies of scholarly journals, primary sources, and books.
LexisNexis Academic	Provides full text of a wide range of newspapers, magazines, government and legal documents, and company profiles from around the world.
ProQuest Databases	Serves as a gateway to a large collection of databases with over 100 billion pages, including the best archives of doctoral dissertations and historical newspapers.

10f Find Sources on the Web

The web offers you some resources for current topics that would be difficult or impossible to find in a library. The key to success is knowing where you are most likely to find current and accurate information about the particular question you are researching, knowing how to access that information, and knowing how to test its reliability (see Chapter 11).

Search engines

Search engines designed for the web work in ways similar to library databases and your library's online catalogue but with one major difference. Databases typically do some screening of the items they list, but search engines potentially take you to everything on the web—millions of pages in all.

Find online government sources

The advanced searches on Google and Yahoo! give you the options of using a string of words to search for sites that contain (1) all the words, (2) the exact phrase, or (3) any of the words, or that exclude (4) certain words. They also allow you to specify the language of the site, the date range, the file format, and the domain. For example, if you want to limit a search for ADHD to Canadian government websites such as Health Canada or U.S. government websites such as the National Institutes of Health, you can specify the domain as .gov; for Canadian federal government websites, use the domain .gc.ca. Statistics Canada (www.statcan.ca) also has a wealth of useful statistical information.

Find online reference sources

Your library's website may have a link to **reference sites**, either on the main page or under a heading such as **research tools**.

Reference sites are usually organized by subject, and you can find resources under the subject heading.

- **Business information** (links to business databases and sites such as *Hoover's* that profile companies)
- **Dictionaries** (including the *Oxford English Dictionary* and various subject dictionaries and language dictionaries)
- **Encyclopedias** (including *Britannica Online* and others)
- **Reference books** (commonly used books such as atlases, almanacs, biographies, handbooks, and histories)

Search interactive media

Several search engines have been developed for interactive media. Facebook and Twitter also have search engines for their sites.

Tips for web searches

Help! My search turned up too many results.

- Try more specific search terms.
- Combine the words with AND.
- Use a phrase within quotation marks or specify "the exact phrase."
- Specify NOT for terms you are not interested in finding.
- Limit the search by a date range.

Help! My search turned up too few results.

- Check your spelling.
- Try broader search terms.
- Use OR instead of AND, or specify "find any of the words."
- Try another index or search engine.

Keep track of web research

You will need the following information to document sources you find on the web.

- Name of the page
- Author if listed
- Sponsoring organization if listed
- Date the site was posted
- Date you visited
- Complete URL

See Section 14e for detailed instructions on how to find the information you need for MLA documentation. See Section 15b for instructions on finding the information you need for APA documentation.

10g Find Multimedia Sources Online

Visual databases and the web give you access to many multimedia sources that were difficult to locate just a few years ago.

Visual databases

Most of the provinces and territories have large collections of photographs and other visual material available on their websites. The Library and Archives Canada website (www.collectionscanada.ca) allows searches for film, video, and sound related to the history of Canada. The Canadian Council of Archives' website provides access to more than 50,000 descriptions of archival records from all the provinces and territories (see Archives Canada (CAIN) via www.cdncouncilarchives.ca).

Find images

The major search engines for images include the following.

- **Bing Images** (www.bing.com/images)
- **Google Images** (images.google.com)
- **Picsearch** (www.picsearch.com)
- **Yahoo! Image Search** (images.search.yahoo.com)

Libraries and museums also offer large collections of images.

Find videos

- **Bing Videos** (www.bing.com/videos)
- **Google Videos** (video.google.com)
- **Yahoo! Video Search** (video.search.yahoo.com)
- **YouTube** (www.youtube.com)

Find podcasts

- **iTunes Podcast Resources** (www.apple.com)
- **PodcastDirectory.com** (http://www.podcastdirectory.com)

Find charts, graphs, and maps

You can find statistical data represented in charts and graphs on many government websites.

- **Statistical Abstract of the United States**
  (www.census.gov/compendia/statab)
- **Google Earth** (earth.google.com)
- **National Geographic Map Machine**
  (mapmachine.nationalgeographic.com)

Respect copyright

Just because images, videos, and other multimedia files are easy to download from the web does not mean that everything is available for you to use. Look for the creator's copyright notice and suggested credit line. This notice will tell you if you can reproduce the multimedia file.

Downloading and inserting images

You will need the following information to document visual sources you find on the web.

- Title of the work
- Author or artist
- Name of the site or archive
- Sponsoring organization if listed
- Date the site was posted
- Date you visited
- Complete URL

Just because images are easy to download from the web does not mean that every image is available for you to use. Look for the image creator's copyright notice and suggested credit line. This notice will tell you if you can reproduce the image. Most images on government websites can be reproduced, but check the copyright restrictions. You should acknowledge the source of any image you use.

Using visuals in a research paper

Here are a few guidelines to keep in mind for incorporating visual sources into your research paper.

- **Use visuals for examples and supporting evidence, not for decoration.**
- **Refer to images and other graphics in the body of your research paper.** Explain in the body of your paper the significance of any image or graphic.
- **Include captions for images and other graphics.**
- **Respect the copyright of visual sources.** You may need to request permission to use a visual from the web. Use public domain material whenever possible.
- **Get complete citation information.** You are required to cite visual sources in your list of works cited just as you are required to cite other sources.

11 | Evaluating Sources

QUICK*TAKE*

- Determine the relevance of sources (see below)
- Evaluate database and print sources (see below)
- Evaluate web sources (see p. 60)

11a Determine the Relevance of Sources

- Does a source you have found address your research question?
- Does a source support or disagree with your working thesis? (You should not throw out work that challenges your views.)
- Does a source add to your content in an important way?
- Is the material you have found persuasive?
- What indications of possible bias do you note in the source?

11b Determine the Reliability of Print and Database Sources

Printed and online materials in your library undergo a review by professional librarians who select them to include in their collections. However, many printed and database sources contain their share of inaccurate, misleading, and biased information. Also, all sources carry the risk of being outdated when you are looking for current information.

Checklist for evaluating database and print sources
Over the years librarians have developed a set of criteria for evaluating sources, and you should apply them in your research.

1. **Source**. Who published the book or article? Enter the publisher's name on Google or another search engine to learn about the publisher. Scholarly books and articles in scholarly journals are

generally more reliable than popular magazines and books, which tend to emphasize what is sensational or entertaining at the expense of accuracy and comprehensiveness.

2. **Author.** Who wrote the book or article? What are the author's qualifications? Enter the author's name on Google or another search engine to learn more about him or her. Does the author represent an organization?

3. **Timeliness.** How current is the source? If you are researching a fast-developing subject such as treating ADHD, then currency is very important, but even historical topics are subject to controversy or revision.

4. **Evidence.** Where does the evidence come from—facts, interviews, observations, surveys, or experiments? Is the evidence adequate to support the author's claims?

5. **Biases.** Can you detect particular biases of the author? How do the author's biases affect the interpretation offered?

6. **Advertising.** For print sources, is advertising a prominent part of the journal or newspaper? How might the ads affect the credibility or the biases of the information that gets printed?

11c Compare Database Sources Versus Web Sources

There is a world of difference between doing a search on library databases through your library's website and doing a general search on the web using Google. Library databases have the advantages of high quality and no commercial intrusion along with the convenience of web delivery. When you search a subject on Google, the results often give you a series of commercial sites selling books and products related to the words you typed in.

	Library database sources	Web sources
Speed	✓ Users can find information quickly	✓ Users can find information quickly
Accessibility	✓ Available 24/7	✓ Available 24/7

	Library database sources	Web sources
Organization	✓ Materials are organized for efficient search and retrieval	Users must look in many different places for information
Consistency and quality	✓ Librarians review and select resources	Anyone can claim to be an "expert," regardless of qualifications
Comprehensiveness	✓ Collected sources represent a wide body of knowledge	No guarantee that the full breadth of an issue will be represented
Permanence	✓ Materials remain available for many years	Materials can disappear or change in an instant
Free of overt bias	✓ Sources are required to meet certain standards of documentation and rigour	Sources are often a soapbox for organizations or individuals with particular agendas
Free of commercial slant	✓ Sources are largely commercial-free	Sources often try to sell you something

11d Evaluate Web Sources

Nearly every large company and political and advocacy organization has a website. We expect these sites to represent the company or the point of view of the organization. Many sites on the web, however, are not so clearly labeled.

Checklist for evaluating web sources

Use these criteria for evaluating websites:

1. **Source.** What organization sponsors the website? Look for the site's owner at the top or bottom of the home page or in the web address. Enter the owner's name on Google or another search engine to learn about the organization. If a website doesn't indicate ownership, then you have to make judgments about who put it up and why.

2. **Author**. Is the author identified? Look for an "About Us" link if you see no author listed. Enter the author's name on Google or another search engine to learn more about the author. Many websites give no information about their authors other than an e-mail address, if that. In such cases it is difficult or impossible to determine the author's qualifications. Be cautious about information on an anonymous site.

3. **Purpose**. Is the website trying to sell you something? Many sites are infomercials that might contain useful information, but they are no more trustworthy than other forms of advertising. Is the purpose to entertain? To inform? To persuade?

4. **Timeliness**. When was the website last updated? Look for a date on the home page. Many web pages do not list when they were last updated; thus you cannot determine their currency.

5. **Evidence**. Are sources of information listed? Any factual information should be supported by indicating where the information came from. Reliable websites that offer information will list their sources.

6. **Biases**. Does the website offer a balanced point of view? Many sites conceal their attitude with a reasonable tone and seemingly factual evidence such as statistics. Citations and bibliographies do not ensure that a site is reliable. Look carefully at the links and sources cited, and peruse the "About Us" link if one is available.

12 | Planning Field Research

QUICK*TAKE*

- Conduct informative interviews (see below)
- Design and administer surveys (see p. 63)
- Make detailed observations (see p. 64)

12a Know What You Can Obtain from Field Research

Even though much of the research you do for post-secondary courses will be secondary research conducted at a computer or in the library, some topics do call for primary research, requiring you to gather information on your own. Field research of this kind can be especially important for exploring local issues.

Be aware that the ethics of conducting field research require you to inform people about what you are doing and why you are gathering information. If you are uncertain about the ethics of doing field research, talk to your instructor.

Three types of field research that can usually be conducted in post-secondary schools are interviews, surveys, and observations.

- **Interviews:** Interviewing experts on your research topic can help build your knowledge base. You can also use interviews to discover what the people most affected by a particular issue are thinking and feeling.
- **Surveys:** Small surveys can often provide insight on local issues.
- **Observations:** Local observations can also be a valuable source of data. For example, if you are researching why a particular office on your campus does not operate efficiently, you might observe what happens when students enter.

12b Conduct Interviews

Before you contact anyone to ask for an interview, think carefully about your goals; knowing what you want to find out through your interviews will help you determine whom to interview and what questions to ask.

- Decide what you want or need to know and who best can provide that information for you.
- Schedule each interview in advance, and let the person know why you are conducting the interview.
- Plan your questions in advance. Write down a few questions and have a few more in mind. Listen carefully so you can follow up on key points.
- Come prepared with a notebook and pencil for taking notes and jotting down short quotations. Record the date, time, place, and subject of the interview. If you want to use a recording device, ask for permission in advance.
- When you are finished, thank your subject and ask his or her permission to get in touch again if you have additional questions.
- When you are ready to incorporate the interview into a paper or project, think about what you want to highlight about the interview and which direct quotations to include.

12c Administer Surveys

Use surveys to find out what groups of people think about a topic. You need to decide what exactly you want to know, then design a survey that will provide that information.

- Write specific questions. To make sure your questions are clear, test them on a few people before you conduct the survey.
- Include one or two open-ended questions, such as "What do you like about X?" "What don't you like about X?" Open-ended questions can be difficult to interpret, but sometimes they turn up information you had not anticipated.
- Decide whom you will need to survey. For example, if you want to claim that the results of your survey represent the views of residents of a dormitory, your method of selecting respondents should give all residents an equal chance to be selected. Don't select only your friends.
- Decide how you will contact participants in your survey. If you are going to mail or e-mail your survey, include a statement about what the survey is for and a deadline for returning it.

- Think about how you will interpret your survey. Multiple-choice formats make data easy to tabulate, but often they miss key information. Open-ended questions will require you to figure out a way to group responses.
- When writing about the results, be sure to include information about who participated in the survey, how the participants were selected, and when and how the survey was administered.

12d Record Observations

Your observations can inform scholarly readers by providing a vivid picture of real-world activity.

- Carry a notebook, tablet, or laptop and make extensive field notes.
- Record details about the context in which your observations occurred.
- Record when you arrived and left, where you were, and exactly what you saw and heard.
- Analyze your observations before you write about them. That is, identify patterns and organize your report according to those patterns.
- Write on one side of your notebook so you can use the facing page to note key observations and analyze your data later.

Consider organizing your observations this way:

- **Title**: Be precise (Forage fish activity in Fiesta Lake August 2010).
- **Description and context**: How did you limit your site or subject? What background do readers need?
- **Record of observations**: Report what you observed in a logical way (operational description, description of parts, cause and effect, examples, analogy, history).
- **Conclusion or summary**: Give readers a framework for understanding your observations. What are your conclusions? Are there questions left unanswered?

13 | Using Sources Ethically and Effectively

QUICKTAKE

- Understand what is considered plagiarism (see below)
- Understand what sources need to be acknowledged (see pp. 67–68)
- Decide when to quote and when to paraphrase (see pp. 70–71)
- Use quotations effectively (see p. 72)
- Use summaries and paraphrases effectively (see pp. 69–70)

Careful documentation of sources is essential to developing knowledge and allows scholars and researchers to build on the work of other scholars and researchers. In Western culture, not acknowledging the quotations or sources you use in your paper is considered plagiarism and often carries a stiff penalty from institutions.

Understand and Recognize Plagiarism

Plagiarism means claiming credit for someone else's intellectual work, no matter whether it's to make money or get a better grade. Intentional or not, plagiarism has dire consequences. Reputable authors have gotten into trouble through carelessness by copying passages from published sources without acknowledging those sources. A number of famous people have had their reputations tarnished by accusations of plagiarism, and several prominent journalists have lost their jobs and careers for copying the work of other writers and passing it off as their own.

Deliberate plagiarism

If you buy a paper on the Internet, copy someone else's paper word for word, or take an article off the web and turn it in as yours, it's plain stealing. Anyone who takes that risk should know that the punishment can be severe—usually failure for the course and sometimes expulsion. Deliberate plagiarism is easy for your instructors to spot because they recognize shifts

in style, and it is easy for them to use search engines to find the sources of work stolen from the web.

Patch plagiarism

The use of the web has increased instances of plagiarism in college. Some students view the Internet as a big free buffet where they can grab anything, paste it into a file, and submit it as their own work. Other students intend to submit work that is their own, but they commit patch plagiarism because they aren't careful in taking notes to distinguish the words of others from their own words.

Original source

The economic advantage that has already begun to accrue to the walkable places can be attributed to three key factors. First, for certain segments of the population, chief among them young "creatives," urban living is simply more appealing; many wouldn't be caught dead anywhere else. Second, massive demographic shifts occurring right now mean that these pro-urban segments of the population are becoming dominant, creating a spike in demand that is expected to last for decades. Third, the choice to live the walkable life generates considerable savings for these households.

—Jeff Speck. *Walkable City: How Downtown Can Save America One Step at a Time.* New York: Farrar, 2012. Print.

Here phrases and an entire sentence highlighted in colour are lifted from the original without quotation marks or acknowledgment of the source.

Patch plagiarism

The economic advantage gained by walkable places can be attributed to three key factors. First, for certain segments of the population, chief among them young "creatives," urban living is simply more appealing; many wouldn't be caught dead anywhere else. Second, young urban professionals are becoming dominant, creating a spike in demand that is expected to last for decades. Third, young professionals have figured out that they can save money by not owning a car.

Avoid Plagiarism

Copying someone else's paper word for word or taking an article off the Internet and turning it in as your own is plagiarism. But if plagiarism also means using the ideas, melodies, or images of someone else without acknowledging them, then the concept is much broader and more difficult to define.

What you don't have to document

Fortunately, common sense governs issues of academic plagiarism. The standards of documentation are not so strict that the source of every fact you cite must be acknowledged. Suppose you are writing about the causes of maritime disasters and you want to know how many people drowned when the *Titanic* sank on the early morning of April 15, 1912. You check the Britannica Online website and find that the death toll was around 1,500. Since this fact is available in many reference works, you would not need to cite Britannica Online as the source.

COMMON ERRORS

Plagiarism and writing in post-secondary education

If you find any of the following problems in your academic writing, it is likely you are plagiarizing someone else's work. Because plagiarism is usually inadvertent, it is especially important that you understand what constitutes using sources responsibly.

- **Missing attribution.** The author of a quotation has not been identified. A lead-in or signal phrase that provides attribution to the source is not used, and no author is identified in the citation.
- **Missing quotation marks**. Quotation marks do not appear around material quoted directly from a source.
- **Inadequate citation.** No page number is given to show where in the source the quotation, paraphrase, or summary is drawn from.
- **Paraphrase relies too heavily on the source.** Either the wording or sentence structure of a paraphrase follows the source too closely.

(Continued on next page)

COMMON ERRORS *(Continued)*

- **Distortion of meaning.** A paraphrase or summary distorts the meaning of the source, or a quotation is taken out of context, resulting in a change of meaning.
- **Missing works-cited entry.** The works-cited section does not include all the works that are cited in the paper.
- **Inadequate citation of images.** A figure or photo appears with no label, number, caption, or citation to indicate the source of the image. If the text includes a summary of data from a visual source, no attribution or citation is given for the graph being summarized.

What you do have to document

For facts that are not easily found in general reference works, statements of opinion, and arguable claims, you should cite the source. You should also cite the sources of statistics, research findings, examples, graphs, charts, and illustrations. When in doubt, always document the source.

 ## Quote Sources Without Plagiarizing

Most people who get into plagiarism trouble lift words from a source and use them without quotation marks. Where the line is drawn is easiest to illustrate with an example. In the following passage, Steven Johnson takes issue with the metaphor of surfing applied to the web:

> Web surfing and channel surfing are genuinely different pursuits; to imagine them as equivalents is to ignore the defining characteristics of each medium. . . . A channel surfer hops back and forth between different channels because she's bored. A web surfer clicks on a link because she's interested.
>
> —Steven Johnson. *Interface Culture: How New Technology Transforms the Way We Create and Communicate.* New York: Harper, 1997, 107–09. Print.

If you were writing a paper or putting up a website that concerned web surfing, you might want to mention the distinction that Johnson makes between channel surfing and surfing on the web. Your options are to paraphrase the source or to quote it directly.

If you quote directly, you must place quotation marks around all words you take from the original:

One observer marks this contrast: "A channel surfer hops back and forth between different channels because she's bored. A web surfer clicks on a link because she's interested" (Johnson 109).

Notice that the quotation is introduced and not just dropped in. This example follows MLA style, where the citation goes outside the quotation marks but before the final period.

Summarize and Paraphrase Sources Without Plagiarizing

Summarize

When you *summarize*, you state the major ideas of an entire source or part of a source in a paragraph or perhaps even a sentence. The key is to put the summary in your own words. If you use words from the source, you have to put those words in quotation marks.

Plagiarized Summary

Steven Johnson argues in *Interface Culture* that the concept of "surfing" is misapplied to the Internet because channel surfers hop back and forth between different channels because they're bored, but web surfers click on links because they're interested.

[Most of the words are lifted directly from the original.]

Acceptable Summary

Steven Johnson argues in *Interface Culture* that the concept of "surfing" is misapplied to the Internet because users of the web consciously choose to link to other sites while television viewers mindlessly flip through the channels until something catches their attention.

Paraphrase

When you *paraphrase*, you represent the idea of the source in your own words at about the same length as the original. You still need to include the reference to the source of the idea. The following example illustrates what is not an acceptable paraphrase.

Plagiarized Summary

Steven Johnson argues that the concept of "surfing" does a terrible injustice to what it means to navigate around the web. What makes the idea of web surfing infuriating is the association with television. Surfing is not a bad metaphor for channel hopping, but it doesn't fit what people do on the web. Web surfing and channel surfing are truly different activities; to imagine them as the same is to ignore their defining characteristics. A channel surfer skips around because she's bored while a web surfer clicks on a link because she's interested (107–09).

Even though the source is listed, this paraphrase is unacceptable. Too many of the words in the original are repeated here, including much or all of entire sentences. When a string of words is lifted from a source and inserted without quotation marks, the passage is plagiarized.

A true paraphrase represents an entire rewriting of the idea from the source.

Acceptable Paraphrase

Steven Johnson argues that "surfing" is a misleading term for describing how people navigate on the web. He allows that "surfing" is appropriate for clicking across television channels because the viewer has to interact with what the networks and cable companies provide, just as the surfer has to interact with what the ocean provides. Web surfing, according to Johnson, operates at much greater depth and with much more consciousness of purpose. Web surfers actively follow links to make connections (107–09).

This paraphrase repeats two words that appeared in the omitted text of the ellipses (*navigate* and *connections*) in the original passage quoted on page 68; otherwise its sentence structure and wording are original, and it accurately conveys the meaning of the source.

Incorporate Quotations, Summaries, and Paraphrases Effectively

The purpose of using sources is to *support* what you have to say, not to say it for you. Next to plagiarism, the worst mistake you can make with sources is to string together a series of long quotations. This strategy leaves your readers wondering whether you have anything to say. If you want to refer to an idea or fact and the original wording is not critical, make the point in your own words. Save direct quotations for language that is memorable or gives the character of the source.

Block quotations

When a direct quotation is long, it is indented from the margin instead of being placed in quotation marks. In MLA style, a quotation longer than four lines should be indented ten spaces. In APA style, a quotation of forty words or more is indented five spaces. In both MLA and APA styles, long quotations are double-spaced, like the rest of the paper. When you indent a long quotation this way, it is called a **block quotation**. You still need to integrate a block quotation into the text of your paper. Block quotations should be introduced by mentioning where they came from. Note three points about form in the block quotation.

- There are no quotation marks around the block quotation.
- Words quoted in the original retain the double quotation marks.
- The page number appears after the period at the end of the block quotation.

It is a good idea to include at least one or two sentences following the quotation to describe its significance to your thesis.

Integrate quotations, summaries, and paraphrases

You should check to see whether all sources are well integrated into the fabric of your paper. Introduce quotations by attributing them in the text:

> Many soldiers who fought for the United States in the U.S.-Mexican War of 1846 were skeptical of American motives, including Civil War hero and future president Ulysses S. Grant, who wrote: "We were sent to provoke a fight, but it was essential that Mexico should commence it."(68)

Summaries and paraphrases likewise need introductions. In the following summary signal phrases make it clear which ideas come from the source. The summary also indicates the stance of Lewis and includes a short quotation that gives the flavour of the source.

> In 2001 it became as fashionable to say the Internet changes nothing as it had been to claim the Internet changes everything just two

years before. In the midst of the Internet gloom, one prominent contrarian has emerged to defend the Internet. Michael Lewis observes in *Next: The Future Just Happened* that it's as if "some crusty old baron who had been blasted out of his castle and was finally having a look at his first cannon had said, 'All it does is speed up balls'" (14). Lewis claims that while the profit-making potential of the Internet was overrated, the social effects were not. He sees the Internet demolishing old castles of expertise along with many traditional relationships based on that expertise.

Use quotations effectively

Quotations are a frequent problem area in research papers. Review every quotation to ensure that each is used effectively and correctly.

- **Limit the use of long quotations.** If you have more than one block quotation on a page, look closely to see if one or more can be paraphrased or summarized.
- **Check that each quotation supports your major points rather than make major points for you.**
- **Check that each quotation is introduced and attributed.** Each quotation should be introduced and the author or title named. Check for verbs that signal a quotation: Smith *claims*, Jones *argues*, Brown *states*.
- **Check that each quotation is properly formatted and punctuated.** Note that each documentation system dictates different rules for formatting block quotations. Consult the assigned documentation system for specific details about spacing and indentation rules.
- **Check that you cite the source for each quotation.** You are required to cite the sources of all direct quotations, paraphrases, and summaries.
- **Check the accuracy of each quotation.** It's easy to leave out words or mistype a quotation. Compare what is in your paper with the original source. If you need to add words to make the quotation grammatical, make sure the added words are in brackets. Use ellipses to indicate omitted words.
- **Read your paper aloud to a classmate or a friend.** Each quotation should flow smoothly when you read your paper aloud. Put a check beside rough spots as you read aloud so you can revise later.

PART 3 Incorporating and Documenting Sources

14 | MLA Documentation

QUICKTAKE

- Use in-text citations in MLA style (see pp. 81–86)
- Create citations in the list of works cited (see pp. 87–108)
- Format a paper in MLA style (see pp. 108–116)

The Modern Language Association (MLA) documentation style is used in the humanities and fine arts. If you have questions that this chapter does not address, consult the *MLA Handbook for Writers of Research Papers,* seventh edition (2009), and the *MLA Style Manual and Guide to Scholarly Publishing,* third edition (2008).

14a Citing Sources in an MLA-Style Project

Writer at Work

Matt Loicano chose to compare two works of dystopic science fiction for his research paper. He wanted to explore the ways in which the authors satirized the economic systems in their futuristic worlds. You can see the complete paper in Section 14m at the end of this chapter.

How to quote and cite a source in the text of an MLA-style paper

Matt searched for a book in the NEOS Library Consortium Catalogue using the search term "dystopian science fiction." He found *The Cambridge Companion to Utopian Literature* in the *Cambridge Collections Online* database.

Name of database

Book title

Date

Book editor

To begin his analysis, Matt decided to quote Gregory Claeys's definition of *dystopia* to show how the term applied to the otherwise opposed societies (one capitalist, one communist).

Matt can either (1) cite Gregory Claeys in the text of his paper with a signal phrase or (2) place the author's name inside parentheses following the quotation (see below). Either with or without the signal phrase, in most cases he would include the page number where he found the quotation inside parentheses.

Author's name in signal phrase

> The main difference between dystopian literature and utopian literature, according to Gregory Claeys, is that "literary dystopia utilizes the narrative devices of literary utopia . . . but predicts that inherently subjective definition of what is 'bad,' or 'less perfect.'" As Claeys later notes, "One person's utopia [is] another's dystopia" (108).

OR

Author's name in parenthetical citation

> The *Cambridge Companion to Utopian Literature* notes the main difference between dystopian literature and utopian literature is that "literary dystopia utilizes the narrative devices of literary utopia . . . but predicts that inherently subjective definition of what is 'bad,' or 'less perfect.'" Moreover, "One person's utopia [is] another's dystopia" (Claeys 108).

If Matt includes a quotation that is four lines or longer, he must double-space and indent the quotation in his paper 1 inch (see example on p. 113).

Include in-text citations for summaries and paraphrases
To show the parallels between Zamyatin's One State in *We* and Soviet Russia, Matt quotes from Christopher Fern's introduction to *We*.

> Unlike H. G. Wells's futuristic world that barely resembles the
> source society, Zamyatin makes the parallels between the world of
> the One State in *We* and Soviet Russia very clear: "While depicting
> a society of the far future, [Zamyatin] clearly takes as his starting
> point Lenin's Socialist Order . . . and project[s] a world where that
> order is now absolute" (Fern 107).

14b Creating the List of Works Cited

Writer at Work

Matt is ready to create an entry for the list of works cited at the end of his paper. He kept a copy of this screenshot from his search of the NEOS Catalogue and made notes about the proper information needed to create the works-cited entry. He used the instructions on the facing page to form the entry.

Matt asked himself a series of questions to create an entry for this source in his list of works cited.

1. What information do I need to pull from this screenshot?

For a source like this article from an online database, he needs to know five things: (1) what type of source it is; (2) the author; (3) the title; (4) the publication information; and (5) information about the online database.

2. How do I find the author's name?

Look for a bold heading that says something like "AUTHOR" or "BYLINE." If more than one author is listed, take note of all names listed.

3. What is the title of my source?

If the title is not immediately evident, look for a heading that says "TITLE" or "HEADLINE."

4. Where do I find the publication information?

The name and date of the periodical are usually listed at the top of the page but sometimes are found at the bottom. In this case the page number is listed beside "SECTION." Publication information for books can be found on the page after the title page at the front of the book.

5. Where do I find the name of the database?

For databases distributed by EBSCO, you have to look for the name of the database. EBSCO is the vendor that sells access to many databases such as *Academic Search Complete*. LexisNexis is the vendor that distributes access to *LexisNexis Academic* and other LexisNexis databases.

Matt listed the information.

AUTHOR	Claeys, Gregory
TITLE OF ARTICLE	"The Origins of Dystopia: Wells, Huxley and Orwell"
PUBLICATION INFORMATION	
Name of publication	The Cambridge Companion to Utopian Literature.
Date of publication	2010
Publisher	Cambridge UP
DATABASE INFORMATION	
Name of database	Cambridge Collections Online
Date the site was accessed	6 Mar. 2012

Then he used the instruction on page 79 to format his citation. You can see Matt's complete list of works cited on page 116 at the end of this chapter.

Loicano 10

Works Cited

Claeys, Gregory. "The Origins of Dystopia: Wells, Huxley and Orwell."
   The Cambridge Companion to Utopian Literature. Ed. Gregory
   Claeys. Cambridge: Cambridge UP, 2010. *Cambridge Collections
   Online*. Web. 6 Mar. 2012.

14c In-Text Citations in MLA Style

Paraphrase, summary, or short quotation

A short quotation takes four lines or fewer in your paper.

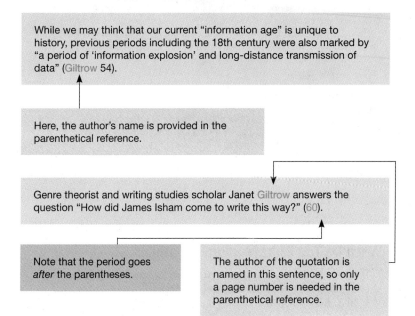

While we may think that our current "information age" is unique to history, previous periods including the 18th century were also marked by "a period of 'information explosion' and long-distance transmission of data" (Giltrow 54).

Here, the author's name is provided in the parenthetical reference.

Genre theorist and writing studies scholar Janet Giltrow answers the question "How did James Isham come to write this way?" (60).

Note that the period goes *after* the parentheses.

The author of the quotation is named in this sentence, so only a page number is needed in the parenthetical reference.

Quotations longer than four lines

The sentence introducing the quotation names the author, so only the page number needs to appear in the parenthetical reference.

Genre theorist and writing studies scholar Janet Giltrow argues that an 18th century fur trader working for the Hudson's Bay Company learned the genre of communication from an outpost through local contexts:

> The rhetorical history of this trader-writer is, inescapably, the history of his colleagues and acquaintances, too, for his ways of writing can be shown to be the outcome of social interaction, rather than schooling, or compliance with convention. As products of and contributions to social interaction, these ways of writing are not approaches to an ideal type but contingent replications, resilient but unenforceable opportunities, and incentives to other, unforeseen speech. (54)

Note that the period appears *before* the parentheses in an indented block quote.

When Do You Provide a Page Number?

- If the source is longer than one page, provide the page number for each quotation, paraphrase, and summary.
- If an online source includes paragraph numbers rather than page numbers, use *par.* with the number.

(Cello, par. 4)

- If the source does not include page numbers, consider citing the work and the author in the text rather than in parentheses.

In a hypertext version of James Joyce's *Ulysses*, . . .

14d Sample In-Text Citations in MLA Style

1. **Author named in your text**

Put the author's name in a signal phrase in your sentence.

> Astrobiologist Ranjit Patel argues that Enceladus, one of Saturn's moons, may have "extraterrestrial life" (3).

2. **Author not named in your text**

> According to Statistics Canada figures, women in 2003 were actually earning "slightly less—2%" than they had earned compared to men in 1995 (Grisson 254).

3. **Work by one author**

The author's last name comes first, followed by the page number. There is no comma.

> (Patel 3)

4. **Work by two or three authors**

The authors' last names follow the order of the title page. If there are two authors, join the names with *and*. If there are three, use commas between the first two names and a comma with *and* before the last name.

> (Francisco, Vaughn, and Lynn 7)

5. **Work by four or more authors**

You may use the phrase *et al.* (meaning "and others") for all names but the first, or you may write out all the names. Make sure you use the same method for both the in-text citations and the works-cited list.

> (Abrams et al. 1653)

6. Work by an unnamed author

Use a shortened version of the title that includes at least the first important word.

> A review in the *New Yorker* of Ryan Adams's new album focuses on the artist's age ("Pure" 25).

"Pure" is in quotation marks because it is the (shortened) title of an article.

7. Work by a group or organization

Treat the group or organization as the author. Identify the group author in the text and place only the page number in the parentheses.

> According to the *Irish Free State Handbook*, published by the Ministry for Industry and Finance, the population of Ireland in 1929 was approximately 4,192,000 (23).

8. Quotations longer than four lines

NOTE: When using indented ("block") quotations—longer than four lines—the period appears *before* the parentheses enclosing the page number.

> In her article "Art for Everybody," Susan Orlean attempts to explain the popularity of painter Thomas Kinkade:
>
>> People like to own things they think are valuable. . . . The high price of limited editions is part of their appeal: it implies that they are choice and exclusive, and that only a certain class of people will be able to afford them. (128)
>
> This same statement could possibly also explain the popularity of phenomena like PBS's *Antiques Roadshow*.

If the source is longer than one page, provide the page number for each quotation, paraphrase, and summary.

9. **Work in an anthology**

Cite the name of the author of the work within an anthology, not the name of the editor of the collection. Alphabetize the entry in the list of works cited by the author, not the editor.

> In "Beard," Melissa Jane Hardie explores the role assumed by Elizabeth Taylor as the celebrity companion of gay actors including Rock Hudson and Montgomery Clift (278-79).

10. **Two or more works by the same author**

Use the author's last name and then a shortened version of the title of each source.

> The majority of books written about coauthorship focus on partners of the same sex (Laird, *Women* 351).

Note that *Women* is italicized because it is the title of a book; if an article were named, quotation marks would be used.

11. **Different authors with the same last name**

Include the initial of the author's first name in the parenthetical reference.

> Web surfing requires more mental involvement than channel surfing (S. Johnson 107).

12. **Two or more sources within the same citation**

If two sources support a single point, separate them with a semicolon.

> (McKibbin 39; Gore 92)

13. **Work quoted in another source**

> National governments have become increasingly what Ulrich Beck, in a 1999 interview, calls "zombie institutions"—institutions which are "dead and still alive" (qtd. in Bauman 6).

14. **Online sources including web pages, podcasts, wikis, tweets, blogs, videos, and other multimedia sources**

MLA prefers that you mention the author in your text instead of putting the author's name in parentheses. In addition, because many online sources do not include page numbers, they are usually named in text rather than in a parenthetical citation, as in the example below.

> Andrew Keen ironically used his own blog to claim that "blogs are boring to write (yawn), boring to read (yawn) and boring to discuss (yawn)."
>
> In a hypertext version of James Joyce's *Ulysses*, . . .

If an online source includes paragraph numbers rather than page numbers, use *par.* with the number.

> (Cello, par. 4)

Multimedia sources (music, film, DVDs, TV programs, interviews) are also usually named in text rather than in a parenthetical citation.

> *House of Flying Daggers* was one of the first feature films to be released on Sony's UMD format for the PSP portable system.

15. **Literary works**

To supply a reference to literary works, you sometimes need more than a page number from a specific edition. Readers should be able to locate a quotation in any edition of the book. Give the page number from the edition that you are using, then a semicolon and other identifying information.

> "Marriage is a house" is one of the most memorable lines in *Don Quixote* (546; pt. 2, bk. 3, ch. 19).

14e   Illustrated Samples and Index of Works Cited in MLA Style

Printed Article

You can find recent issues of printed scholarly journals and popular magazines in your library's periodicals room. Older issues are shelved on the stacks with books. Use your library's online catalogue to find the location.

Scholarly journals usually list the publication information at the top or bottom of the first page. Popular magazines often do not list volume and issue numbers. You can find the date of publication on the cover.

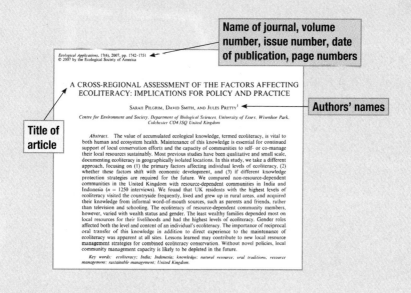

Name of journal, volume number, issue number, date of publication, page numbers

Authors' names

Title of article

Pilgrim, Sarah, David Smith, and Jules Pretty. "A Cross-Regional Assessment of the Factors Affecting Ecoliteracy: Implications for Policy and Practice." *Ecological Applications* 17.6 (2007): 1742-51. Print.

Author's Name

The author's last name comes first, followed by a comma and the first name.

For two or more works by the same author, see page 85.

Title of Article

Use the exact title and put it inside quotation marks. If a book title is part of the article's title, italicize the book title.

Publication Information

Name of journal or newspaper
Italicize the title of the journal or newspaper.

Abbreviate the title if it commonly appears that way.

Volume, issue, and page numbers
For scholarly journals give the volume number and issue number. Place a period between the volume and issue numbers: "55.3" indicates volume 55, issue 3.

Some scholarly journals use issue numbers only.

Give the page numbers for the entire article, not just the part you used.

Medium of publication
Print.

Printed Book

Use your library's online catalogue to locate printed books on the library's shelves. Find the copyright date on the copyright page, which is on the back of the title page. Use the copyright date for the date of publication, not the date of printing.

Author → BRUCE STOVEL

Book title → Jane Austen & Company

Collected Essays

Editor → NORA FOSTER STOVEL | EDITOR

Stovel, Bruce. *Jane Austen & Company: Collected Essays*. Ed. Nora Foster Stovel. Edmonton: U of Alberta P, 2011. Print.

Author's or Editor's Name

The author's last name comes first, followed by a comma and the first name.

For edited books, put the abbreviation *ed.* after the name, preceded by a comma:

Kavanagh, Peter, ed.

Book Title

Use the exact title, as it appears on the title page (not the cover).

Italicize the title.

Publication Information

Place of publication
If more than one city is given, use the first.

Publisher
Omit words such as *Publisher* and *Inc.*

For university presses, use *UP*:

New York UP

Shorten the name. For example, shorten *W. W. Norton & Co.* to *Norton*.

Date of publication
Give the year as it appears on the copyright page.

If no year of publication is given, but can be approximated, put a *c.* ("circa") and the approximate date in brackets: [c. 1999].

Otherwise, put n.d. ("no date"): Toronto: U of Toronto P, n.d.

Medium of publication
Print.

Library Database Publication

You will find library databases linked off your library's website (see page 52). A few databases including Google Scholar are available to everyone, but most library databases are password protected if you access them off campus.

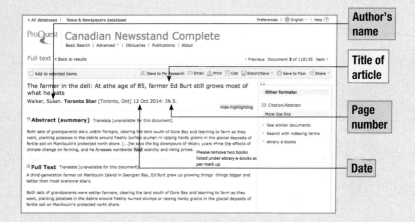

Take Note

Don't confuse the name of the vendor—the company that sells access to the database—with the name of the database. For example, EBSCO or EBSCO Host is not the name of a database but the name of the vendor that sells access to databases such as *Academic Search Complete*.

Walker, Susan. "The Farmer in the Dell: At the Age of 85, Farmer
Ed Burt Still Grows Most of What He Eats." *Toronto Star*
12 Oct. 2014: IN5. *ProQuest*. Web. 14 Jan. 2015.

Author's Name

The author's last name comes first, followed by a comma and the first name. For two or more works by the same author, see page 85.

Title of Source

Use the exact title and put it inside quotation marks. If a book title is part of the article's title, italicize the book title.

Publication Information for an Article

Name of journal or newspaper
Italicize the title of the journal or newspaper. Abbreviate the title if it commonly appears that way.

Volume, issue, date, and page numbers
List the same information you would for a print item. If there are no page numbers, put *n. pag.* where the page numbers would ordinarily go.

Database Information

Name of the database
Italicize the name of the database, followed by a period.

Medium of publication
For online database sources, the medium of publication is *Web*.

Date of access
List the date you accessed the source (day, month, year).

To create a citation for a publication found using your library database, start with the format for a print citation. Replace the word *Print* at the end with the name of the database, the medium (*Web*), and the date you accessed the source.

Most databases allow you to search by document type, such as scholarly journal, newspaper article, financial report, legal case, or abstract. Use these categories to identify the type of publication.

Web Publication

Name of site →

Name of publication →

Title →

Author name →

When Do You List a URL?

MLA style no longer requires including URLs of web sources. URLs are of limited value because they change frequently and they can be specific to an individual search. Include the URL as supplementary information only when your readers probably cannot locate the source without the URL.

Hyland, Theresa. "Multilingual Learners in the Writing Centre:
    Some Musings on Negotiated Practice." *Inkshed* 31 (Jan.
    2014). Web. 4 Apr. 2014.

Author's Name

Authorship is sometimes hard to discern for online sources. If you know the author or creator, follow the rules for books and journals.

If the only authority you find is a group or organization, list its name after the date of publication or last revision.

Title of Source

Place the title of the work inside quotation marks if it is part of a larger website.

Untitled works may be identified by a label (e.g., *Home page, Introduction*). List the label in the title slot without quotation marks or italics.

Italicize the name of the overall site if it is different from the work. The name of the overall website will usually be found on its index or home page.

On websites that are updated, list the version if you find it (e.g., *Vers. 1.2*).

Publication Information for Web Sources

List the publisher's or sponsor's name followed by a comma. If it isn't available, use *N.p.*

List the date of publication by day, month, and year if available. If you cannot find a date, use *n.d.*

Give the medium of publication (*Web*).

List the date you accessed the site by day, month, and year.

14f Journals, Magazines, Newspapers, and Other Print Sources

JOURNAL AND MAGAZINE ARTICLES

16. Article by one author

> Graves, Roger. "Why Students Struggle with Writing: What to Do about It." *University Affairs* 54.8 (2013): 37. Print.

17. Article by two or three authors

> Marcoux, Sarah, Liv Catherine Marken, and Stan Yu. "Establishing Peer Mentor-Led Writing Groups in Large First-Year Courses." *Collected Essays on Learning and Teaching* 5 (2012): 55-64. Print.

18. Article by four or more authors

You may use the phrase *et al.* (meaning "and others") for all authors but the first, or you may write out all the names.

> Breece, Katherine E., et al. "Patterns of mtDNA Diversity in Northwestern North America." *Human Biology* 76.1 (2004): 33-54. Print.

19. Article by an unknown author

> "Light Box." *Time* 28 Jan. 2013: 6-7. Print.

20. Monthly or seasonal magazines

Use the month (or season) and year in place of the volume number. Abbreviate the names of all months except May, June, and July.

> Bodnar, Chris. "Software Tools for the Small Farm." *British Columbia Organic Grower* Summer (2013): 6.

21. **Weekly or biweekly magazines**

Give both the day and month of publication, as listed on the issue.

George, Lianne. "It's Not Just a Car Anymore . . . It's a Home."
    Maclean's 27 Feb. 2006: 20-25. Print.

DIFFERENT TYPES OF PAGINATION

22. **Article in a scholarly journal**

List the volume and issue numbers after the name of the journal.

Duncan, Mike. "Whatever Happened to the Paragraph?" *College
    English* 69.5 (2007): 470-95. Print.

23. **Article in a scholarly journal that uses only issue numbers**

If a journal begins each issue on page 1, list the issue number after the
name of the journal.

McCall, Sophie. "Double Vision Reading." *Canadian Literature* 194
    (2007): 95-97. Print.

REVIEWS, EDITORIALS, LETTERS TO THE EDITOR IN A JOURNAL OR MAGAZINE

24. **Review**

If there is no title, just name the work reviewed.

Mendelsohn, Daniel. "The Two Oscar Wildes." Rev. of *The
    Importance of Being Earnest*, dir. Oliver Parker. *New York
    Review of Books* 10 Oct. 2002: 23-24. Print.

25. **Letter to the editor**

Patai, Daphne. Letter. *Harper's* Dec. 2001: 4. Print.

26. **Editorial**

Putting the Cat Among the Pigeons. *Edmonton Journal* 27 Jan.
    2015: A12. Print.

NEWSPAPER ARTICLES

27. Article by one author

Simons, Paula. "Irrationality the Most Dangerous Infection." *Edmonton Journal* 8 Apr. 2014, final ed.: A5. Print.

28. Article by two or three authors

Chazen, Guy, and Dana Cimilluca. "BP Amasses Cash for Oil-Spill Costs." *Wall Street Journal* 26 June 2010: A1. Print.

29. Article by an unknown author

"Balmy Winter Backs Global-Warming Theory." *The Record* [Kitchener-Waterloo] 14 Mar. 2006: A1+. Print.

30. Article that continues to a nonconsecutive page

Add a plus sign after the number of the first page.

Kaplow, Larry, and Tasgola Karla Bruner. "U.S.: Don't Let Taliban Forces Flee." *Austin American-Statesman* 20 Nov. 2001, final ed.: A1+. Print.

NEWSPAPER REVIEWS, EDITORIALS, LETTERS TO THE EDITOR

31. Review

Eisenthal, Bram. "Stephen King Turns Cellphone Users into Zombies." Rev. of *Cell* by Stephen King. *Montreal Gazette* 18 Feb. 2006: H1. Print.

32. Letter to the editor

Lapointe, Kenneth. "Ojibway Conservation Not 'Twisted Priority.'" Letter. *Windsor Star* 18 Mar. 2006: A6. Print.

33. Editorial

> "Putting the Cat Among the Pigeons." *Edmonton Journal* 27 Jan.
> 2015: A12. Print.

If the editorial is unsigned, put the title first.

GOVERNMENT DOCUMENTS

34. Government document

> *House of Commons Debates.* Cat. no. X3-391/9E. Vol. 141, No. 9.
> 25 Apr. 2006. Print.

DISSERTATIONS

35. Published dissertation or thesis

> Mason, Jennifer. *Civilized Creatures: Animality, Cultural Power, and
> American Literature, 1850-1901.* Diss. U of Texas at Austin,
> 2000. Ann Arbor: UMI, 2000. 9992865. Print.

Books

ONE AUTHOR

36. Book by one author

> Mayer-Schönberger, Viktor. *Delete: The Virtue of Forgetting in the
> Digital Age.* Princeton: Princeton UP, 2009. Print.

37. Two or more books by the same author

In the entry for the first book, include the author's name. In the second entry, substitute three hyphens and a period for the author's name. List the titles of books by the same author in alphabetical order.

Krakauer, Jon. *Into the Wild*. New York: Villard, 1996. Print.

---. *Where Men Win Glory: The Odyssey of Pat Tillman*. New York: Doubleday, 2009. Print.

MULTIPLE AUTHORS

38. Book by two or three authors

The second and subsequent authors' names appear first name first.

Burger, Edward B., and Michael Starbird. *Coincidences, Chaos, and All That Math Jazz*. New York: Norton, 2006. Print.

39. Book by four or more authors

You may use the phrase *et al.* (meaning "and others") for all authors but the first, or you may write out all the names. Use the same method in the in-text citation as you do in the works-cited list.

Damrosch, David, et al. *The Longman Anthology of World Literature*. Compact ed. New York: Longman, 2008. Print.

ANONYMOUS AND GROUP AUTHORS

40. Book by an unknown author

Begin the entry with the title.

The Canadian Encyclopedia. 2nd ed. Toronto: McClelland, 1988. Print.

41. Book by a group or organization

Treat the group as the author of the work.

United Nations. *The Charter of the United Nations: A Commentary*. New York: Oxford UP, 2000. Print.

PARTS OF BOOKS

42. Introduction, foreword, preface, or afterword

Strong-Boag, Veronica. Introduction. *In Times Like These*. By Nellie
McClung. 1915. Toronto: U of Toronto P, 1972. vii-xx. Print.

43. Selection in an anthology or edited collection

Sedaris, David. "Full House." *The Best American Nonrequired Reading
2004*. Ed. Dave Eggers. Boston: Houghton, 2004. 350-58. Print.

44. More than one selection from an anthology or edited collection

Multiple selections from a single anthology can be handled by creating a complete entry for the anthology and shortened cross-references for
individual works in that anthology.

Adichie, Chimamanda Ngozi. "Half of a Yellow Sun." Eggers 1-17.

Eggers, Dave, ed. *The Best American Nonrequired Reading 2004*.
Boston: Houghton, 2004. Print.

Sedaris, David. "Full House." Eggers 350-58.

45. Article in a reference work

"Utilitarianism." *The Columbia Encyclopedia*. 6th ed. 2001. Print.

THE BIBLE AND OTHER SACRED TEXTS

46. Sacred text

The New Oxford Annotated Bible. Ed. Bruce M. Metzger and Roland
E. Murphy. New York: Oxford UP, 1991. Print.

Use a period to separate the chapter and verse in the in-text note:
(John 3.16)

EDITIONS, TRANSLATIONS, AND ILLUSTRATED BOOKS

47. Book with an editor—focus on the editor

Lewis, Gifford, ed. *The Big House of Inver*. By Edith Somerville and Martin Ross. Dublin: Farmar, 2000. Print.

48. Book with an editor—focus on the author

Somerville, Edith, and Martin Ross. *The Big House of Inver*. Ed. Gifford Lewis. Dublin: Farmar, 2000. Print.

49. Book with a translator

Mallarmé, Stéphane. *Divagations*. 1897. Trans. Barbara Johnson. Cambridge: Harvard UP, 2007. Print.

50. Second or subsequent edition of a book

Hawthorn, Jeremy, ed. *A Concise Glossary of Contemporary Literary Theory*. 3rd ed. London: Arnold, 2001. Print.

51. Illustrated book or graphic narrative

After the title of the book, give the illustrator's name, preceded by the abbreviation *Illus.* If the emphasis is on the illustrator's work, place the illustrator's name first, followed by the abbreviation *illus.*, and list the author after the title, preceded by the word *By*.

Strunk, William, Jr., and E. B. White. *The Elements of Style Illustrated*. Illus. Maira Kalman. New York: Penguin, 2005. Print.

MULTIVOLUME WORKS

52. One volume of a multivolume work

Samuel, Raphael. *Theatres of Memory*. Vol. 1. London: Verso, 1999. Print.

14h Library Database Sources

Give the print citation followed by the name of the database in italics, the medium (*Web*), and the date you accessed the database. You do not need to list the URL of common library databases.

53. Scholarly journal article from a library database

Greco, Albert N., & Aiss, Chelsea G. "University Presses in the Twenty-first Century: The Potential Impact of Big Data and Predictive Analytics on Scholarly Book Marketing." *Journal of Scholarly Publishing*, 46(2015): 105. proquest.com. Web. 27 Jan. 2015.

54. Magazine article from a library database

Jeevan. "The Education Track." *Digital Learning* 01 2012. *ProQuest*. Web. 8 Apr. 2014.

55. Article with unknown author from a library database

"Dicing with Data: Facebook, Google and Privacy." *Economist* 22 May 2010, U.S. ed.: 16. *LexisNexis Academic*. Web. 15 Sept. 2013.

56. Newspaper article from a library database

Franciane, Valerie. "Quarter Is Ready to Rock." *Times-Picayune* [New Orleans] 3 Apr. 2007: 1. *LexisNexis Academic*. Web. 23 Jan. 2014.

57. Legal case from a library database

Bilski v. Kappos. 561 US 08-964. Supreme Court of the US. 28 June 2010. *LexisNexis Academic*. Web. 28 June 2014.

Web Sources and Other Online Sources

WEBSITES

58. **Page on a website**

   The basic format for citing a web page includes the author or editor, the title of the page, the title of the site (in italics), the sponsor or publisher of the site, the date of publication, the medium (*Web*), and the date you accessed the site.

> Deterding, Sebastian. "Research." *Coding Conduct: Persuasive Design for Digital Media*. Web. 8 Apr. 2014.

59. **Entire website**

> Deterding, Sebastian. *Coding Conduct: Persuasive Design for Digital Media*. Web. 8 Apr. 2014.

PUBLICATIONS ON THE WEB

60. **Publication by a known author**

> Mims, Christopher. "Everything I need to Know about Management I Learned from Playing Dungeons and Dragons." *Quartz News Blog*. Quartz.com, 29 Jan. 2014. Web. 8 Apr. 2014.

61. **Publication by a group or organization**

   If a work has no author's or editor's name listed, begin the entry with the title.

> "State of the Birds." *Audubon*. Natl. Audubon Society, 2012. Web. 19 Aug. 2013.

62. **Publication on the web with print publication data**

Include the print publication information. Then give the name of the website or database in italics, the medium of publication (*Web*), and the date of access (day, month, and year).

> Kirsch, Irwin S., et al. *Adult Literacy in America*. Darby: Diane,
> 1993. *Google Scholar*. Web. 30 Oct. 2010.

PERIODICALS ON THE WEB

63. **Article in a scholarly journal on the web**

Some scholarly journals are published on the web only. List articles by author, title, name of journal in italics, volume and issue number, and year of publication. If the journal does not have page numbers, use *n. pag.* in place of page numbers. Then list the medium of publication (*Web*) and the date of access (day, month, and year).

> Fleckenstein, Kristie. "Who's Writing? Aristotelian Ethos and
> the Author Position in Digital Poetics." *Kairos* 11.3 (2007):
> n. pag. Web. 6 Apr. 2014.

64. **Article in a newspaper on the web**

List the name of the newspaper in italics, followed by a period and the publisher's name. Follow the publisher's name with a comma. The first date is the date of publication; the second is the date of access.

> Boyer, Suzanne. "Some Youth Are Already Trying to Stay in
> Motion." *Moose Jaw Times-Herald*. Transcontinental, 14 Mar.
> 2006. Web. 18 Mar. 2006.

65. **Article in a popular magazine on the web**

> Brown, Patricia Leigh. "The Wild Horse Is Us." *Newsweek*.
> Newsweek, 1 July 2008. Web. 12 Dec. 2013.

DIGITAL BOOKS, ARCHIVES, AND GOVERNMENT PUBLICATIONS

66. Document within an archive on the web

Give the print information, then the title of the scholarly project or archive in italics, the medium of publication (*Web*), and the date of access (day, month, and year).

Jane Austen Entry. *The Orlando Project: A History of Women's Writing in the British Isles.* Edmonton: U of Alberta, n.d. Web. 1 July 2005.

67. Government publication

If you cannot locate an author's name for the document, give the name of the government and the agency that published it.

Canada. Canada Revenue Agency. *2010-2011 Annual Report to Parliament.* Canada Revenue Agency, 2 Nov. 2011. Web. 31 Mar. 2012.

UNEDITED ONLINE SOURCES

68. Wiki entry

Wiki content is written collaboratively; thus no author is listed. Because the content on a wiki changes frequently, wikis are not considered reliable scholarly sources.

"Snowboard." *Wikipedia.* Wikimedia Foundation, 2014. Web. 30 Jan. 2014.

69. E-mail and text messaging

Give the name of the writer, the subject line, a description of the message, the date, and the medium of delivery (*E-mail, Text message*).

Ballmer, Steve. "A New Era of Business Productivity and Innovation." Message to Microsoft Executive E-mail. 30 Nov. 2006. E-mail.

70. Posting to a discussion list

Give the name of the writer, the subject line, the name of the list in italics, the publisher, the date of the posting, the medium (*Web*), and the date of access.

> Dobrin, Sid. "Re: ecocomposition?" *Writing Program Administration*.
> Arizona State U, 19 Dec. 2008. Web. 5 Jan. 2014.

71. **Course home page**

> Graves, Roger. "WRS 302: Proposal Writing." Course home page.
> U of Alberta, Fall 2013. Web. 8 Apr. 2014.

72. **Blog entry**
    If there is no sponsor or publisher for the blog, use *N.p.*

> Arrington, Michael. "Think Before You Voicemail." *TechCrunch*.
> N.p., 5 July 2008. Web. 10 Sept. 2013.

73. **Twitter**

> Graves, Roger (rogergraves). "Rhetoric and Mathematics. http://
> wp.me/p1pKxy-87." 1 June 2014, 10:24 am. Tweet.

74. **Facebook**
    MLA does not have an official style yet. However, the following entry
    is derived from MLA rules.

> Globe and Mail. The Benefits of an Urban Forest: New Report Breaks
> Down the Value of a Tree to Toronto Residents. http://bit.ly/
> 1jfXywr. Facebook posting. 9 June 2014. Web. 16 June 2014.

14j Visual Sources

75. **Cartoon or comic strip**

> Trudeau, G. B. "Doonesbury." Comic strip. *Washington Post* 21 Apr.
> 2008. C15. Print.

76. **Advertisement**
    Begin with the name of the advertiser or product, then the word
    Advertisement.

Nike. Advertisement. ABC. 8 Oct. 2010. Television.

77. **Map, graph, or chart**

Specify *Map*, *Graph*, or *Chart* after the title.

Greenland. Map. Vancouver: International Travel Maps, 2004. Print.

VISUAL SOURCES ON THE WEB

78. **Photograph on the web**

Include the photographer, title of the image, and the date, then the name of the website, the medium (*Web*), and the date of access.

Swansburg, John. *The Illinois Monument at the Vicksburg National Military Park*. 2010. *Slate.com*. Web. 18 Oct. 2013.

79. **Video on the web**

Video on the web often lacks a creator and a date. Begin the entry with a title if you cannot find a creator. Use *n.d.* if you cannot find a date.

Wesch, Michael. *A Vision of Students Today*. *YouTube*. YouTube, 2007. Web. 28 May 2013.

80. **Work of art on the web**

Include the artist, title of the work in italics, and the date. For works found on the web, omit the medium but include the location or museum, then add the name of the website, the medium (*Web*), and the date of access.

Carr, Emily. *Totem Poles, Kitseukla*. 1912. Vancouver Art Gallery. Web. 15 Mar. 2012.

81. **Map on the web**

Edmonton, Alberta. Map. *Google Maps*. Google, 2014. Web. 8 Apr. 2014.

82. **Cartoon or comic strip on the web**

Tomorrow, Tom. "Modern World." Comic strip. *Huffington Post*. HuffingtonPost.com, 2 Jan. 2014. Web. 20 Jan. 2014.

14k **Multimedia Sources**

83. Podcast

> Ghomeshi, Jian. "Cultural Fallout of Quebec Election, 'Dirty Daddy'
> Bob Saget, Rwanda and Reconciliation." CBC Radio, 8 Apr.
> 2014. Web. 8 Apr. 2014.

84. Film

Begin with the title in italics. List the director, the distributor, the
date, and the medium. Other data, such as the names of the screenwriters
and performers, is optional.

> *Wanted*. Dir. Timur Bekmambetov. Perf. James McAvoy, Angelina
> Jolie, and Morgan Freeman. Universal, 2008. Film.

85. DVD

> *No Country for Old Men*. Dir. Joel Coen and Ethan Coen. Perf. Tommy
> Lee Jones, Javier Bardem, and Josh Brolin. Paramount, 2007. DVD.

86. Television or radio program

> "Wild Horses." *Heartland*. Perf. Amber Marshall, Graham Wardle,
> and Michelle Morgan. CBC. 11 Mar. 2012. Television.

87. Telephone interview

> Zuckerberg, Mark. Telephone interview. 5 Mar. 2013.

14l **Sample Research Paper with MLA Documentation**

Formatting a Research Paper in MLA Style

MLA offers these general guidelines for formatting a research paper.

- **Use white, 8½-by-11-inch paper.** Don't use colored or lined paper.
- **Double-space everything—the title, headings, body of the paper,
  quotations, and works-cited list.** Set the line spacing on your word
  processor for double spacing and leave it there.

- **Put your last name and the page number at the top of every page, aligned with the right margin, ½ inch from the top of the page.** Your word processor has a header command that will automatically put a header with the page number on every page.
- **Specify 1-inch margins.** One-inch margins are the default setting for most word processors.
- **Do not justify (make even) the right margin.** Justifying the right margin throws off the spacing between words and makes your paper harder to read. Use the left-align setting instead.
- **Indent the first line of each paragraph ½ inch (5 spaces).** Set the paragraph indent command or the tab on the ruler of your word processor at ½ inch.
- **Use the same readable typeface throughout your paper.** Use a standard typeface such as Times New Roman, 12 point.
- **Use block format for quotations longer than four lines.** See page 71.
- **MLA does not require a title page.** Unless your instructor asks for a separate title page, put 1 inch from the top of the page your name, your instructor's name, the course, and the date on separate lines. Centre your title on the next line. Do not underline your title or put it inside quotation marks.

Formatting the Works Cited in MLA Style

- **Begin the works-cited list on a new page.** Insert a page break with your word processor before you start the works-cited page.
- **Centre "Works Cited" on the first line at the top of the page.**
- **Double-space all entries.**
- **Alphabetize each entry by the last name of the author or, if no author is listed, by the first content word in the title (ignore *a, an, the*).**
- **Indent all but the first line in each entry ½ inch.**
- **Italicize the titles of books and periodicals.**
- **If an author has more than one entry, list the entries in alphabetical order by title. Use three hyphens in place of the author's name for the second and subsequent entries.**

    Murphy, Dervla. *Cameroon with Egbert*. Woodstock: Overlook, 1990. Print.

    ---. *Full Tilt: Ireland to India with a Bicycle*. London: Murray, 1965. Print.

- **Go through your paper to check that each source you have used is included in the works-cited list.**

14m Sample Research Paper and Works-Cited Page

Include your last name and page number as page header, beginning with the first page, 1/2" from the top.*

↑1"

Loicano 1 ↑1/2"

Matt Loicano

Professor Churchill

Comparative Literature 242

16 October 2011

Centre the title. Do not underline the title, put it inside quotation marks, or type it in all capital letters.

Satiric Dystopia in *The Time Machine* and *We*

H. G. Wells's *The Time Machine* and Yevgeny Zamyatin's *We* are both widely considered to be classic works of dystopic science fiction. Both novels extrapolate from the social and political climates in which they were written to paint a bleak, disturbing picture of the world rooted in the society of the times. The satirical societies presented in these works serve as warnings against continuing further down the same path. While *We* aims to draw attention to the problems of totalitarian communism in early 20th century Russia, *The Time Machine* points out flaws in the class-based capitalism of post-Industrial Revolution Europe. Both works aim to draw attention to the problems of the societies that inspired them, but the dystopic worlds used by the authors to illustrate these problems are very different due to the conflicting ideologies of the satirized societies.

Loicano's thesis appears at the end of the first paragraph.

The two worlds explored in *We* and *The Time Machine* are both considered dystopias, despite their vast differences, because of the abstract and somewhat ambiguous definitions of what constitutes a utopia or dystopia. The etymology of the words *utopia* (*ouk:* "not" + *topos:* "place," alternatively *eu:* "good" +

Specify 1" margins all around. Double-space everything.

←— 1" —→

↕ 1"

---

*Portions shown in this paper are adjusted to fit the space limitations of this book. Follow the actual dimensions discussed in this book and your instructor's directions.

Loicano 2

topos: "place") and *dystopia* (*dus:* "bad, abnormal,
diseased" + *topos:* "place") is itself fairly general
(Churchill). Darko Suvin defines a utopia to be a
"community where sociopolitical institutions, norms,
and individual relationships are organized according to
a more perfect principle than in the author's
community," and he derives his definition of a
dystopia by substituting a "less perfect principle" into
his definition of utopia (49). Similarly, the main
difference between dystopian literature and utopian
literature according to Gregory Claeys is that "literary
dystopia utilizes the narrative devices of literary
utopia . . . but predicts that inherently subjective
definition of what is 'bad,' or 'less perfect.'" As Claeys
later notes, "One person's utopia [is] another's
dystopia" (108). This subjective nature of dystopia
allows the societies of both *We* and *The Time Machine*
to be viewed as dystopic, even though the societies
they satirize are based on the opposing principles of
communism and capitalism.

    In *The Time Machine*, H. G. Wells constructs a
futuristic society projected from the society of
post-Industrial Revolution Britain. The
commercialization of the steam engine in 1781 spurred
the Industrial Revolution, replacing the water wheel as
the main source of power in factories by 1800 and
allowing the factories to move into the more densely
populated cities where workers were abundant
(Liebedowski). The abundance of workers allowed
factories to pay low wages by the hour while the

Cite publications within the text by the name of the author (or authors).

Indent each paragraph ½ inch.

Loicano 3

factory owners became rich (Liebedowski). By the end
of the 19th century, this system of capitalism had
created an enormous economic and social gap between
the rich aristocracy and the poor workers, which
formed the basis for the dystopic society of the Eloi
and Morlocks in *The Time Machine* (Cook 100). When
describing his theory of the origin of the Eloi and
Morlocks, the Time Traveller himself states:

". . . proceeding from the problems of our own age, it
seemed clear as daylight to me that the gradual
widening of the present merely temporary and social
difference between the Capitalist and the Labourer,
was the key to the whole position" (Wells 24). Wells's
experiences with capitalism heavily influenced his
thoughts about the future of civilization, and hence
the characteristics of his present-day world that he
chose to satirize in the futuristic society of *The Time
Machine*.

The society of the Eloi and Morlocks contains
many characteristics that satirize aspects of the
society of Wells's time. The Time Traveller implies that
the Morlocks' adaptation to living underground is the
logical extension of the life of a factory worker,
asking: "Even now, does not an East-end worker live in
such artificial conditions as practically to be cut off
from the natural surface of the earth?" (Wells 24). He
further suggests that the working poor will be literally
forced underground by the "exclusive tendency of
richer people . . . [which] is already leading to the
closing . . . of considerable portions of the surface of

Sources not
identified with
an author are
referenced in
text by title.

Loicano 4

the land" (24). To make it clear that the resulting society is clearly dystopic and not an aristocrat's utopia, the Time Traveller mentions the extinction of farm animals and reveals the Morlocks' cannibalism of the aristocratic Eloi (14, 30). To be unequivocal about the need for social change, the Time Traveller describes the cannibalistic Eloi and Morlock society as the "logical conclusion [of] the industrial system of to-day" (24). By giving the futuristic society characteristics extrapolated from Wells's present day, and then introducing a universally detested concept such as cannibalism, Wells makes a scathingly critical statement about capitalism, the direction in which his society is headed, and the need for change.

Give page numbers for paraphrases as well as direct quotations.

Yevgeny Zamyatin also creates a satiric dystopia in *We* for the purpose of criticizing the society of his time. In 1917, with Russia heavily engaged in the First World War, bread riots in Petrograd (now St. Petersburg) escalated into socialist protests opposing the war and the monarchy (Pavlovic). Soldiers and workers rebelled, and the Russian Civil War began between the Bolshevik (majority) Red Army and the anti-Bolshevik White Army (Pavlovic). As the Bolshevik party consolidated power, dissenting views were increasingly suppressed. It was this progression toward an oppressive society that Yevgeny Zamyatin sought to avert.

Loicano 5

Unlike H. G. Wells's futuristic world that barely resembles the source society, Zamyatin makes the parallels very clear between the world of the One State in *We* and Soviet Russia: "While depicting a society of the far future, [Zamyatin] clearly takes as his starting point Lenin's Socialist Order . . . and project[s] a world where that order is now absolute" (Fern 107). The control of the One State extends to every aspect of citizens' lives, including aspects that Zamyatin's society would likely consider extremely intimate. The protagonist, D-503, prompts the reader to realize how easily privacy is taken for granted when he wonders about the state of the olden days: "Wasn't it absurd that the state (it dared to call itself a state!) could leave sexual life without any semblance of control?" (Zamyatin 13). Zamyatin is extrapolating from the oppressive Soviet regime past the point most people in his society would be comfortable with to reveal the impact of the oppressive Bolshevik regime on their lives and to dissuade people from supporting further oppression.

Zamyatin also criticizes the impact of the oppressive regime on the lives and freedoms of citizens in other ways. He uses the secret police of the One State, the Operational Section, several times to illustrate the dangers of state control. The protagonist, D-503, rationalizes the existence of the Operational Section thus:

> There were some fools who compared the
> Section to the ancient Inquisition, but that

Loicano 6

is as absurd as equating a surgeon performing
a tracheotomy with a highwayman; both may
have the same knife in their hands, both do
the same thing—cut a living man's
throat—yet one is a benefactor, the other
a criminal. (80)

By using a faulty analogy to rationalize the
existence of a secret police that tortures citizens to
extract information using a "Gas Bell," Zamyatin refutes
an important strategy of Soviet propaganda. He leads
the reader to draw the conclusion that the secret police
in an oppressive regime (like that of the Bolsheviks)
should not exist and that change is needed in the
author's present-day society.

Both *The Time Machine* and *We* satirize the
societies of the era in which they were written by
extrapolating from the then-current political and social
climates to arrive at a disturbing dystopia. However,
the futuristic dystopias that the authors create, as well
as the societies they are criticizing, are based on
opposing principles of capitalism and communism.
While *The Time Machine* makes it clear that capitalism
results to some degree in a "cannibalistic" stratified
class system, *We* argues that the equality of communism
enforced through totalitarian means is an equally
dystopic system. As Fátima Vieira writes, "Since it is
impossible for [man] to build an ideal society, then he
must be committed to the construction of a better one"
(17). In the end, both works succeed in suggesting that
social change is necessary.

Quotations of more than four lines should be indented one inch. Do not use quotation marks. Introduce block quotations rather than just dropping them into the text.

Loicano 7

Works Cited

Churchill, Belinda. "Alternate Society." Course Notes
for Comparative Literature 242: Science Fiction.
U of Alberta, Edmonton, 27 Sept. 2011. Print.

Claeys, Gregory. "The Origins of Dystopia: Wells, Huxley
and Orwell." Introduction. *The Cambridge
Companion to Utopian Literature*. Ed. Claeys.
Cambridge: Cambridge UP, 2010. *Cambridge
Collections Online*. Web. 16 Oct. 2011.

Cook, Paul. Afterword. *The Time Machine*. H. G. Wells.
1992. Web. 16 Oct. 2011.

Fern, Christopher. *Narrating Utopia: Ideology, Gender,
Form in Utopian Literature*. Liverpool: Liverpool UP,
1999. Print.

Liebedowski, Lech. "Industrial Revolution." Course
Notes for History 391: History of Technology.
U of Alberta, Edmonton. 11 Sept. 2011. Print.

Pavlovic, Srdja. "The Bolsheviks." Course Notes for
History 295: History of 20th Century Warfare. U of
Alberta, Edmonton. 20 July 2011. Print.

Suvin, Darko. *Metamorphoses of Science Fiction: On the
Poetics and History of a Literary Genre*. New Haven:
Yale UP, 1979. Print.

Vieira, Fátima. "The Concept of Utopia." *The Cambridge
Companion to Utopian Literature*. Ed. Gregory
Claeys. Cambridge: Cambridge UP, 2010. *Cambridge
Collections Online*. Web. 18 Oct. 2011.

Wells, H. G. *The Time Machine*. 2011. PDF file.

Zamyatin, Yevgeny. *We*. Trans. Mirra Ginsburg. New York:
Avon, 1987. Print.

Centre
"Works Cited"
on a new page.

Double-space all
entries. Indent all
but the first line
in each entry by
1/2 inch.

Alphabetize entries
by the last names
of the authors or
by the first
important word in
the title if no
author is listed.

Italicize the titles
of books and
periodicals.

Go through your
text and make
sure that all the
sources you have
used are in the list
of works cited.

15 | APA Documentation

QUICK*TAKE*

- Use in-text citations in APA style (see pp. 119–121)
- Create citations in the list of references (see pp. 122–133)
- Format a paper in APA style (see pp. 134–140)

Social sciences disciplines, including political science, linguistics, psychology, sociology, and education, frequently use the American Psychological Association (APA) documentation style. For a detailed treatment of APA style, consult the *Publication Manual of the American Psychological Association*, sixth edition (2010).

In-Text Citations in APA Style

APA style emphasizes the date of publication. When you cite an author's name, always include the date of publication.

> Zukin (2004) observes that teens today begin to shop for themselves at age 13 or 14, "the same age when lower-class children, in the past, became apprentices or went to work in factories" (p. 50).

If the author's name is not mentioned in the sentence, the reference looks like this:

> One sociologist notes that teens today begin to shop for themselves at age 13 or 14, "the same age when lower-class children, in the past, became apprentices or went to work in factories" (Zukin, 2004, p. 50).

See Section 15g, pages 139–140, for a sample reference list.

Quotations 40 words or longer

Orlean (2001) has attempted to explain the popularity of the painter Thomas Kinkade:

> People like to own things they think are valuable. . . . The high price of limited editions is part of their appeal; it implies that they are choice and exclusive, and that only a certain class of people will be able to afford them. (p. 128)

The sentence introducing the quotation names the author.

Note that the period appears before the parentheses in an indented "block" quote.

The date appears in parentheses immediately following the author's name.

15b Sample In-Text Citations in APA Style

When Do You Need to Give a Page Number?

- Give the page number for all direct quotations, when available. For electronic sources without page numbers, give the paragraph number when available (e.g., para. 4) or cite the heading and the number of the paragraph following it (e.g., "Mandatory Labelling," para. 2).
- For other sources that do not include page numbers, it is preferable to reference the work and the author in the text (e.g., "In Wes Anderson's 1998 film *Rushmore*, . . .").
- APA encourages but does not require you to provide page numbers when paraphrasing or referring to ideas in other works.

1. **Author named in your text**

Astrobiologist Ranjit Patel (2006) argues that Enceladus, one of Saturn's moons, may have "extraterrestrial life" (p. 3).

2. Author not named in your text

> According to Statistics Canada figures in 2006, women in 2003 were actually earning "slightly less—2%" than they had earned compared to men in 1995 (Grisson, 2006, p. 254).

3. Work by a single author

> (Patel, 2006, p. 3)

4. Work by two authors

> (Deane & Ganobcsik-Williams, 2012, p. 190)

5. Work by three to five authors
The authors' last names follow the order of the title page:

> (Marcoux, Marken, & Yu, 2012, p. 56)

Subsequent references can use the first name and *et al.*

> (Marcoux et al., 2012, p. 59)

6. Work by six or more authors
Use the first author's last name and *et al.* for all in-text references:

> (Bazerman et al., 2010, p. 49)

7. Work by a group or organization
Identify the group author in the text and place only the page number in the parentheses:

> Defined by the National Commission on Writing (2004) as a *threshold skill* (p. 3), the ability to write well is among the most important skill sets required in the modern workforce.

8. Work by an unknown author
Use a shortened version of the title (or the full title if it is short) in place of the author's name. Capitalize all key words in the title. If it is an article title, place it in quotation marks.

> ("Derailing the Peace Process," 2003, p. 44)

9. Two works by one author with the same copyright date

Assign the dates letters (*a*, *b*, etc.) according to their alphabetical arrangement in the references list.

> The majority of books written about coauthorship focus on
> partners of the same sex (Graves, 2012a, p. 197).

10. Two or more sources within the same sentence

Place each citation directly after the statement it supports.

> Some surveys report an increase in homelessness rates (Alford,
> 2004) while others chart a slight decrease (Rice, 2003a) . . .

If you need to cite two or more works within the same parentheses, list them in the order they appear in the references list and separate them with a semicolon.

> (Alford, 2004; Rice, 2003a)

11. Work quoted in another source

Name the work and give a citation for the secondary source.

> Miller's work (as cited in Artemeva, 2006)

12. Quotations 40 words or longer

Indent long quotations ½ inch and omit quotation marks. Note that the period appears before the parentheses in an indented "block" quote.

> Orlean (2001) has attempted to explain the popularity of the
> painter Thomas Kinkade:
>
> > People like to own things they think are valuable. . . . The
> > high price of limited editions is part of their appeal; it
> > implies that they are choice and exclusive, and that only a
> > certain class of people will be able to afford them. (p. 128)

15c Books and Nonperiodical Sources in APA-Style References List

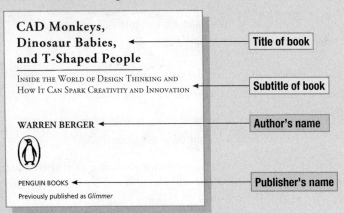

CAD Monkeys,
Dinosaur Babies,
and T-Shaped People ◄—————— **Title of book**

INSIDE THE WORLD OF DESIGN THINKING AND
HOW IT CAN SPARK CREATIVITY AND INNOVATION ◄—— **Subtitle of book**

WARREN BERGER ◄—————————————— **Author's name**

PENGUIN BOOKS ◄——————————————— **Publisher's name**

Previously published as *Glimmer*

TITLE PAGE

Copyright date ——————►

COPYRIGHT PAGE

Berger, W. (2009). *CAD monkeys, dinosaur babies, and T-shaped people: Inside the world of design thinking and how it can spark creativity and innovation.* New York: Penguin.

Author's or Editor's Name

The author's last name comes first, followed by a comma and the author's initials.

If an editor, put the abbreviation *Ed.* in parentheses after the name.

Kavanagh, P. (Ed.).

Book Title

Italicize or underline the title.

Capitalize only the first word, proper nouns, and the first word after a colon.

If the title is in a foreign language, copy it exactly as it appears on the title page.

Year of Publication

Give the year the work was copyrighted in parentheses.

If no year of publication is given, write *n.d.* ("no date") in parentheses:

Smith, S. (n.d.).

If it is a multivolume edited work, published over a period of more than one year, put the span in parentheses:

Smith, S. (1999–2001).

Publication Information

Place of publication
List the city and province or state abbreviation. If the publisher is a university named for a province or state, omit the province or state abbreviation.

For publications outside of North America, spell out the city and country names (Paris, France).

If more than one city is given on the title page, list only the first.

Publisher's name
Do not shorten or abbreviate words like *University* or *Press*. Omit words such as *Co., Inc.,* and *Publishers.*

Sample references for books

13. Book by one author

> Gladwell, M. (2013). *David and Goliath: Underdogs, misfits, and the art of battling giants*. New York, NY: Little, Brown.

For edited works, use the abbreviation *Ed.* in parentheses.

> Rasgon, N. L. (Ed.). (2006). *The effects of estrogen on brain function*. Baltimore, MD: Johns Hopkins University Press.

14. Two or more books by the same author
Arrange according to the date, with the earliest publication first.

> Harris, R. S. (1976). *A history of higher education in Canada, 1663–1960*. Toronto, ON: University of Toronto Press.
> Harris, R. S. (1988). *English studies at Toronto: A history*. Toronto, ON: University of Toronto Press.

15. Book by two authors

> Lindhout, A., & Corbett, S. (2013). *A house in the sky: A memoir*. New York, NY: Scribner.

For edited works, use (Eds.) after the names.

> Lunsford, A. A., & Ouzgane, L. (Eds.). (2004). *Crossing borderlands: Composition and postcolonial studies*. Pittsburgh, PA: University of Pittsburgh Press.

16. Book by eight or more authors
List the first six authors' names, insert three ellipsis points, and finish with the last author's name.

> Anders, K., Child, H., Davis, K., Logan, O., Petersen, J., Tymes, J., . . . Green, R.

17. **Book by an unknown author**

Survey of developing nations. (2003). New York, NY: Justice for All Press.

18. **Book by a group or organization**

Canadian Diabetes Association. (2005). *Living with diabetes.* Toronto, ON: Dorling Kindersley.

19. **Chapter in an edited collection**

Boyaton, D. (2010). Behaviorism and its effect upon learning in schools. In G. Goodman (Ed.), *The educational psychology reader: The art and science of how people learn* (pp. 49–66). New York, NY: Peter Lang.

20. **Article in a reference work**

Viscosity. (2001). *The Columbia encyclopedia* (6th ed.). New York, NY: Columbia University Press.

21. **Government document**

When the author and publisher are identical, use the word *Author* as the name of the publisher.

Health Canada. (2001). *Assessment report of the Canadian Food Inspection Agency activities related to the safety of aquaculture products* (Cat. H39-577/2001E). Ottawa, ON: Author.

22. **Religious or classical text**

Reference entries are not required for major classical works or classical religious texts such as the Bible, but in the first in-text citation, identify the edition used.

John 3.16 (Modern Phrased Version)

15d Periodical Sources In APA-Style References List

Name of journal, volume, issue number, date

Title of article

Authors' names

Abstract

Publication information

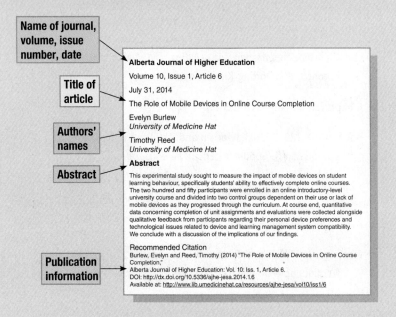

Alberta Journal of Higher Education

Volume 10, Issue 1, Article 6

July 31, 2014

The Role of Mobile Devices in Online Course Completion

Evelyn Burlew
University of Medicine Hat

Timothy Reed
University of Medicine Hat

Abstract

This experimental study sought to measure the impact of mobile devices on student learning behaviour, specifically students' ability to effectively complete online courses. The two hundred and fifty participants were enrolled in an online introductory-level university course and divided into two control groups dependent on their use or lack of mobile devices as they progressed through the curriculum. At course end, quantitative data concerning completion of unit assignments and evaluations were collected alongside qualitative feedback from participants regarding their personal device preferences and technological issues related to device and learning management system compatibility. We conclude with a discussion of the implications of our findings.

Recommended Citation
Burlew, Evelyn and Reed, Timothy (2014) "The Role of Mobile Devices in Online Course Completion,"
Alberta Journal of Higher Education: Vol. 10: Iss. 1, Article 6.
DOI: http://dx.doi.org/10.5336/ajhe-jesa.2014.1.6
Available at: http://www.lib.umedicinehat.ca/resources/ajhe-jesa/vol10/iss1/6

FIRST PAGE OF ARTICLE

Burlew, E., & Reed, T. (2014). The role of mobile devices in online course completion. *Alberta Journal of Higher Education, 10*(1), Article 6. doi:http://dx.doi.org/10.5336/ajhe˜jesa.2014.1.6

Author's Name

Each author's last name comes first, followed by the author's initials.

Join two authors' names with a comma and an ampersand.

Title of Article

Do not use quotation marks. If there is a book title within the article title, italicize it.

The first word of the title, the first word of the subtitle, and any proper nouns in the title are capitalized.

Date of Publication

Give the year the work was published in parentheses.

Most popular magazines are paginated per issue. These periodicals might have a volume number, but they are more often referenced by the season or date of publication.

Publication Information

Name of journal
Italicize the journal name.

All nouns, verbs, and pronouns, and the first word of the title are capitalized. Do not capitalize any article, preposition, or coordinating conjunction unless it is the first word of the title or subtitle.

Put a comma after the journal name.

Italicize the volume number and follow it (leaving no space) with the issue number in parentheses followed by a comma.

Page numbers
See sample references on pp. 138–139 for examples of different types of pagination.

Digital Object Identifiers (DOI) must be included in references when available. If you include a DOI, no other source or publication information is needed.

Sample references for periodical sources

23. Article by one author

Haiek, L. N. (2012). Compliance with baby-friendly policies and practices in hospitals and community health centres in Quebec. *Journal of Human Lactation, 30*(2), 343–358. doi: 10.1177/0890334412448477

24. Article by multiple authors

Chalmers, B., O'Brien, B., & Royale, C. (2012). Rates of interventions in labor and birth across Canada: Findings of the Canadian maternity experiences survey. *Birth,* doi: 10.1111/j.1523-536X.2012.00549.x *39*(3), 203–210.

25. Article by an unknown author

The net is where the kids are. (2003, May 10). *Business Week,* 44.

26. Article in a journal with continuous pagination

Engen, R., & Steen, S. (2000). The power to punish: Discretion and sentencing reform in the war on drugs. *American Journal of Sociology, 105,* 1357–1395.

27. Article in a journal paginated by issue

Davis, J. (1999). Rethinking globalisation. *Race and Class, 40*(2/3), 37–48.

28. Monthly publications

Sherman, A. J. (2014, March). Prime time for veggies. *Vegetarian Times, 40*(4), 52–55.

29. Newspaper article

Simons, P. (2014, April 8). Irrationality the most dangerous infection. *Edmonton Journal,* p. A5.

15e Online Sources in APA-Style References List

Journal title

Title of the article

Author

Volume, page, and DOI

Date

Tenenbaum, D. J. (2005). Global warming: Arctic climate:
The heat is on. *Environmental Health Perspectives, 113,* A91.
doi:10.1289/ehp.113–a91a

Author's Name or Organization

Authorship is sometimes hard to discern for online sources. if you do have an author or creator to cite, follow the rules for periodicals and books.

If the only authority you find is a group or organization, list its name as the author.

Dates

Give the date the site was produced or last revised (sometimes the copyright date) after the author.

Title of Page or Article

Websites are often made up of many separate pages or articles. Each page or article on a website may or may not have a title.

URL and DOI

If the article has a DOI (digital object identifier), give the DOI in numeric or URL form after the title.

If the article does not have a DOI, copy the Web address exactly as it appears in your browser window. You can even copy and paste the address into your text for greater accuracy.

Break a URL at the end of a line *before* a mark of punctuation. Do not insert a hyphen.

Vergolini, L. (2011). Does economic vulnerability affect social cohesion? Evidence from a comparative analysis. *Canadian Journal of Sociology, 36*(1). Retrieved from http://ejournals .library.ualberta.ca/index.php/CJS/

Author's Name, Associated Institution, or Organization

Authorship is sometimes hard to discern for online sources. If you do have an author or creator to cite, follow the rules for periodicals and books.

If the only authority you find is a group or organization, list its name as the author.

If the author or organization is not identified, begin the reference with the title of the document.

Dates

List the date the site was produced or last revised, after the author. This date might be just a year.

If the content is likely to change, also list the date you accessed the site. Place this second date just before the URL. If the content is unlikely to change, such as that of a journal article or book, including the retrieval date is not necessary.

Name of Site and Title of Page or Article

Use the same information as you would for a printed source, if available. Give as much information as needed to help others locate the source.

Websites are often made up of many separate pages or articles. If you are citing a page or article that has a title, treat the title like an article in a periodical. Otherwise, treat the name of the website itself as you would a book.

Many online periodicals use a digital object identifier (DOI), which provides a permanent link to the text. If an article has a DOI, use it instead of a URL in the citation.

If a journal article does not have a DOI, give the URL of the homepage of the journal. If the material would be hard to find, for example, a newsletter of a government agency, give the exact URL.

The name of a website will usually be found on its index or homepage. If you cannot find a link back to the homepage, look at the address for clues. You can work your way backward through the URL, deleting sections (separated by slashes) until you come to a home- or index page.

If there is no title for the website, list it by author or creator. If it is a personal homepage, place the word *Homepage* after the name of the owner of the page.

DOI or URL

If including a DOI or a complete URL, copy it exactly as it appears in your browser window.

Note that there are no angle brackets around the URL or DOI and no period after it.

Sample references for online sources

30. Online publication by a known author

Alexander, K. (2005). Liminal identities and institutional positioning: On becoming a "writing lady" in the academy. *Inkshed, 22*(3), 5–16. Retrieved from http://www.stthomasu.ca/inkshed/

31. Online publication by a group or organization

Canadian Curling Association. (2014). Policy statement and guidelines on discrimination and harassment. Retrieved from http://www.curling.ca/programs-and-services/

32. Online article in a scholarly journal, with DOI

Hall, P. V., & Khan, A. J. (2008). Differences in high-tech immigrant earnings and wages across Canadian cities. *Canadian Geographer, 52*, 271–290. doi:10.1111/j.1541-0064.2008.00213.x

33. Online article in a scholarly journal, no DOI

Greenleaf, W. J., Frieda, K. L., Foster, D. A. N., Woodside, M. T., & Block, S. M. (2008, February 1). Direct observation of hierarchical folding in single riboswitch aptamers. *Science, 319*, 630–633. Retrieved from http://www.sciencemag.org

34. Online article in a newspaper

Thomson, G. (2014, April 17). Updating homophobic Marriage Act no slam dunk. *Edmonton Journal.* Retrieved from http://www.edmontonjournal.com/

35. Article in an online magazine

Mann, C. C. (2014, March 25). Renewables aren't enough: Clean coal is the future. *Wired.* Retrieved from http://www.wired.com/

36. Online government publication

> Health Canada. (2009). *A statistical profile on the health of First Nations in Canada: Determinants of health, 1999 to 2003* (Cat. H34-193/1-2008). Retrieved from http://www.hc-sc.gc.ca/fniah-spnia/alt_formats/fnihb-dgspni/pdf/pubs/aborig-autoch/2009-stats-profil-eng.pdf

37. Weblog entry

> Albritton, C. (2004, May 19). Greetings from Baghdad [Weblog post]. *Back to Iraq.* Retrieved from http://www.back-to-iraq.com/

38. Twitter

> Graves, R. [rogergraves]. (2014, June 1). Rhetoric and mathematics. http://wp.me/p1pKxy-87. [Tweet]. Retrieved from https://twitter.com/rogergraves

39. Facebook

> Globe and Mail. (2014, June 9). The benefits of an urban forest: New report breaks down the value of a tree to Toronto residents. http://bit.ly/1jfXywr. [Facebook status update]. Retrieved from https://www.facebook.com/theglobeandmail

15f Visual, Computer, and Multimedia Sources in APA-Style References List

40. Television program

> Burgess, M., & Green, M. (Writers). (2004). Irregular around the margins [Television series episode]. In D. Chase (Producer), *The Sopranos.* New York, NY: HBO.

41. Film, video, or DVD

> Jackson, P. (Director). (2013). The hobbit: The desolation of Smaug [Motion picture]. United States: Warner Brothers.

15g　Sample Research Paper and References

Running head: HOW THE MEDIA DEPICT NURSING　　1

How the Media Depict Nursing

Impacts Stereotypes and Nursing Practice

Danielle Mitchell

University of Alberta

*Portions shown in this paper are adjusted to fit the space limitations of this book. Follow the actual dimensions discussed in this book and your instructor's directions.

Continue the
running head
on all pages.

Do not indent
the first line
of the abstract.

The abstract
appears on a
separate page
with the title
Abstract
centred at
the top.

Abstract

The misperceptions of nursing in popular media include nurses as unprofessional and as intellectually incapable of being independent and critical thinkers, which, in turn, affects nursing practice. Since the 1960s, nurses have been seen in many roles that depict them as simple-minded, drug addicted, and sexual props for physicians. This diminished view of nurses in the media does have an effect on society's view of nursing as a profession. To close the gap between nurses' depiction in the media and what nurses actually do will require effort from associations such as the Canadian Nurses Association (CNA) and the College & Association of Registered Nurses of Alberta (CARNA) as well as from nurses themselves. The regulatory bodies can launch campaigns, indicating the significance of nurses and what their jobs truly entail. By taking a proactive role, negative stereotypes can be minimized, solving problems induced by media bias.

The abstract
should be a brief
(120 words or
fewer) summary
of your paper's
argument.

How the Media Depict Nursing Impacts
Stereotypes and Nursing Practice

The term *media* is defined as the "main means of mass communication" ("Media," n.d.). In today's society, the media play a large part in everyday life. From the drive to work to sitting at a restaurant, it is hard to avoid topics that are in the media. Nursing is no exception. Nursing has been portrayed in the media in many different ways, but rarely is there a portrayal that depicts a nurse's true role. This is rather disconcerting due to all the progress and effort made by many strong, intelligent nurses such as Florence Nightingale, Mary Agnes Snively, and Jean I. Gunn (among others) to advance the image of nursing as intellectual and professional (Potter, Perry, Ross-Kerr, & Wood, 2010). The misrepresented roles of nurses in popular media do have an effect on society's perception of nurses. For nursing to be considered a professional position in today's culture, the static and inaccurate image of nursing must be drastically rebranded. The misperceptions of nursing in the media include nurses as unprofessional and intellectually incapable of being independent and critical thinkers, which, in turn, affects nursing practice. Nurses must get actively involved to correct this image, which is seen in movies and on television.

Centre your title at the beginning of the body of your paper. If it runs to 2 lines, double-space it.

In a parenthetical citation, use & instead of *and* when listing more than one author.

HOW THE MEDIA DEPICT NURSING   8

primary school children were less likely to choose nursing as a career based on media stereotypes of nurses (Summers, 2010).

Spear (2010) summarizes it well by saying that although shows such as *Nurse Jackie, HawthoRNe,* and *Mercy* often portray their main characters, who are nurses, in a good light, there are still many inaccuracies in the media regarding nursing. To close the gap between the depiction of nurses in the media and what nurses actually do will require effort from associations such as CNA and CARNA, as well as from nurses themselves. The regulatory bodies can launch information campaigns to show the significance of nurses and what their jobs truly entail. Nurses have to stop reinforcing their own stereotypes in saying they are "just nurses" (Cabaniss, 2011, p. 117). They must also work with the media to ensure accurate portrayals of nurses and the nursing profession (Stanley, 2008, p. 94). By taking this proactive role, negative stereotypes can be minimized, solving problems induced by media bias.

The Nursing Image

Nursing stereotypes in the media are ever-present and need to be addressed. The media portrayal of nurses as unprofessional, sexual props needs to be abolished for nurses to become a respected, professional occupation in the eyes of the public. As well, the depiction of nurses as unintelligent needs to be addressed; it indicates to the

If you include the author's name in the text, include the publication year in parentheses immediately after it. If necessary, include the page number in parentheses with the abbreviation *p.* following the citation.

HOW THE MEDIA DEPICT NURSING   9

public that nurses do not hold a vital role in healthcare.
Knowledge-based practices must become evident in popular
media for this stereotype to be dissolved. Nursing has been
facing these stereotypes for decades. Images project
demeaning characteristics and reduce public confidence in
nurses (Kalisch & Kalisch, 1982, p. 264). Nurses, along with
their associations, must become more involved to rebuild the
media's image of nursing. The media are a strong and powerful
source of information. Society must be careful not to stereotype
nurses based on how the media portray them: seemingly
harmless ideas can turn into a completely inaccurate image.

HOW THE MEDIA DEPICT NURSING   10

Centre
References
at the top.

Alphabetize
entries by last
name of the
first author.

Indent all but
the first line
of each entry.

                              References

Cabaniss, R. (2011). Educating nurses to impact change
        in nursing's image. *Teaching and Learning in Nursing,
        6*, 112–118. doi:10.1016/j.teln.2011.01.003

Canadian Nurses Association. (2011a). *Registered nurses
        and baccalaureate education*. Retrieved from
        http://www.cna-nurses.ca/cna/nursing/education
        /baccalaureate/default_e.aspx

Canadian Nurses Association. (2011b). *Standards and
        best practices*. Ottawa, ON: Author. Retrieved from
        http://www.cna-nurses.ca/CNA/practice/standards
        /default_e.aspx

HOW THE MEDIA DEPICT NURSING 11

Davis, P. (2011). *Understanding your regulatory college and professional association*. Edmonton, AB: College Association of Registered Nurses of Alberta. Retrieved from https://vista4.srv.ualberta.ca/webct /urw/1c5122011.tp0/cobaltMainFrame.dowebct

Gordon, S., & Nelson, S. (2005). An end to angels. *American Journal of Nursing, 105*(5), 62–69.

Kalisch, P. A., & Kalisch, B. J. (1982). Nurses on prime-time television. *American Journal of Nursing, 82*, 264–270. Retrieved from http://www.jstor .org/stable/3463069

Media. [n.d]. In *Oxford Dictionaries Online*. Retrieved from http://oxforddictionaries.com/definition/media ?rskey=p7YaEJ&result=2

Potter, P. A., Perry, A. G., Ross–Kerr, J. C., & Wood, M. J. (2010). *Canadian fundamentals of nursing*. Toronto, ON: Moseby/Elsevier.

Spear, H. J. (2010). TV nurses: Promoting a positive image of nursing? *Journal of Christian Nursing, 27*, pp. 218–221.

Stanley, D. J. (2008). Celluloid angels: A research study of nurses in feature films 1900–2007. *Journal of Advanced Nursing, 64*(1), 84–95. doi:10.1111 /j.1365-2648.2008.04793.x

Summers, S. (2010, September 9). The image of nursing: Does nursing's media image matter? *Nursing Times*. Retrieved from http://www.nursingtimes.net /nursing-practice/clinical-specialisms/educators /the-image-of-nursing-does-nursings-media-image -matter/5019099.article

Double-space all entries.

HOW THE MEDIA DEPICT NURSING   12

The Truth About Nursing. (2009). *Nurse Jackie:* The
henchman of god. *The Truth About Nursing.*
Retrieved from http://www.truthaboutnursing.org
/news/2009/jun/08_jackie.html

The Truth About Nursing. (2010a). *Grey's Anatomy:* Right
away doctor. *The Truth About Nursing.* Retrieved from
http://www.truthaboutnursing.org/news/2010
/nov/greys.html

The Truth About Nursing. (2010b). *Private Practice:* I got
in. *The Truth About Nursing.* Retrieved from
http://www.truthaboutnursing.org/news/2010
/aug/2009-10_pp.html

The Truth About Nursing. (2011). Reviews of television
series featuring nurses. *The Truth About Nursing.*
Retrieved from http://www.truthaboutnursing
.org/media/tv

Go through your text and make sure that everything you have cited, except for personal communication, is in the list of references.

Formatting the References in APA Style

- **Begin the references on a new page.** Insert a page break with your word processor before you start the references page.
- **Centre "References" on the first line at the top of the page.**
- **Double-space all entries.**
- **Alphabetize each entry by the last name of the author or, if no author is listed, by the first content word in the title (ignore *a, an, the*).**
- **Indent all but the first line in each entry ½ inch.**
- **Italicize the titles of books and periodicals.**
- **Go through your paper to check that each source you have used (except personal communication) appears in the list of references.**

16 | CMS Documentation

QUICK*TAKE*

- Use footnotes or endnotes for print sources in CMS style (see pp. 143–144)
- Use footnotes or endnotes for online sources in CMS style (see pp. 151–154)

Writers in business, social sciences, fine arts, and humanities often use the *Chicago Manual of Style (CMS)* method of documentation. CMS guidelines allow writers a clear way of using footnotes and endnotes for quotations, summaries, and paraphrases. If you have further questions, consult the complete CMS style manual, *The Chicago Manual of Style*, sixteenth edition (Chicago: University of Chicago Press, 2010).

16a The Elements of CMS Documentation

CMS describes two systems of documentation, one similar to APA and the other a style that uses footnotes or endnotes, which is the focus of this chapter. In the footnote style, CMS uses a superscript number directly after any quotation, paraphrase, or summary. Notes are numbered consecutively throughout the text. This superscript number corresponds to either a footnote, which appears at the bottom of the page, or an endnote, which appears at the end of the text.

> In *Canadian Women: A History*, Prentice and colleagues note ironically that the Upper Canada seduction law of 1837 aimed to protect the interests of fathers rather than masters, and it "ignored" the rights of the young women involved.[1]

Note

> 1. Alison Prentice et al., *Canadian Women: A History* (Toronto: Harcourt Brace Jovanovich, 1988), 93.

Bibliography

> Prentice, Alison, Paula Bourne, Gail Cuthbert Brandt, Beth Light, Wendy Mitchinson, and Naomi Black. *Canadian Women: A History*. Toronto: Harcourt Brace Jovanovich, 1988.

Footnote and endnote placement

Footnotes appear at the bottom of the page on which each citation appears. **Endnotes** are compiled at the end of the text on a separate page titled *Notes*.

CMS bibliography

Because footnotes and endnotes in CMS format contain complete citation information, a separate list of references is optional.

16b   Books and Nonperiodical Sources in CMS Style

Big Bear   ⟵   **Title of book**

by RUDY WIEBE   ⟵   **Author's name**

With an Introduction by
John Ralston Saul

SERIES EDITOR

EXTRAORDINARY
CANADIANS   ⟵   **Publisher's imprint**

TITLE PAGE

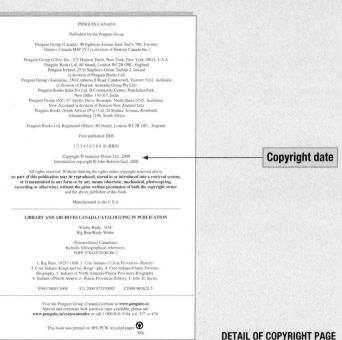

PENGUIN CANADA

Published by the Penguin Group

Penguin Group (Canada), 90 Eglinton Avenue East, Suite 700, Toronto,
Ontario, Canada M4P 2Y3 (a division of Pearson Canada Inc.)

Penguin Group (USA) Inc., 375 Hudson Street, New York, New York 10014, U.S.A.
Penguin Books Ltd, 80 Strand, London WC2R 0RL, England
Penguin Ireland, 25 St Stephen's Green, Dublin 2, Ireland
(a division of Penguin Books Ltd)
Penguin Group (Australia), 250 Camberwell Road, Camberwell, Victoria 3124, Australia
(a division of Pearson Australia Group Pty Ltd)
Penguin Books India Pvt Ltd, 11 Community Centre, Panchsheel Park,
New Delhi- 110 017, India
Penguin Group (NZ), 67 Apollo Drive, Rosedale. North Shore 0745, Auckland,
New Zcooland (a division of Pearson New Zealand Ltd)
Penguin Books (South Africa) (Pty) Ltd, 24 Sturdee Avenue, Rosebank,
Johannesburg 2196, South Africa

Penguin Books Ltd, Registered Offices: 80 Strand, London WC2R 0RL, England

First published 2008

1 2 3 4 5 6 7 8 9 10 (RRD)

Copyright © Jackpine House Ltd., 2008
Introduction copyright © John Ralston Saul, 2008   ⟵   **Copyright date**

All rights reserved. Without limiting the rights under copyright reserved above,
**no part of this publication may be reproduced, stored in or introduced into a retrieval system,
or transmitted in any form or by any means (elecronic, mechanical, photocopying,
recording or otherwise), without the prior written permission of both the copyright owner**
and the above publisher of this book.

Manufactured in the U.S.A.

LIBRARY AND ARCHIVES CANADA CATALOGUING IN PUBLICATION

Wiebe, Rudy, 1934-
Big Bear/Rudy Wiebe.

(Extraordinary Canadians)
Includes bibliographical references.
ISBN 978-0-670-06786-2

I. Big Bear, 1825?-1888. 2. Cree Indians-1'l2irie Provinces--History.
3. Cree Indians-Kings and rul--Biogr--phy. 4. Cree Indians-Prairie Provine-
Biography. 5. Indians of North Amereia-Prairie Provinces-Biography.
6. Indians ofNorth Americo- Prairie Provinces-lliStory. 1. Title. II. Series.

E99.C88B5 2008   971.2004'973230092   C2008-902622-5

Visir the Penguin Group (Canada) website at **www.penguin.ca**
Special and corporate bulk purchase rates available; please see
www.penguin.ca/corporatesales or call 1-800-810-3104, ext. 477 or 474

This book was printed on 30% PCW recycled paper ♻
30%

DETAIL OF COPYRIGHT PAGE

Note

1. Rudy Wiebe, *Big Bear* (Toronto: Penguin, 2008), 15.

Bibliography

Wiebe, Rudy. *Big Bear*. Toronto: Penguin, 2008.

Author's or Editor's Name

- *Note:* the author's name is given in normal order.
- *Bibliography:* give the author's last name first. If an editor, put *ed.* after the name.

Book Title

- Use the exact title, as it appears on the title page (not the cover).
- Italicize the title.
- Capitalize all nouns, verbs, adjectives, adverbs, and pronouns, and the first word of the title and subtitle.

Publication Information

In a note, the place of publication, publisher, and year of publication are in parentheses.

Place of publication
- Add the province or state's abbreviation or country when the city is not well known (*Brandon, MB*) or ambiguous (*London, ON,* or *London, UK*).
- If more than one city is given on the title page, use the first.

Publisher's name
- Omit an initial *The* and abbreviations such as *Co., Publishing Co., Inc., Ltd.,* or *S.A.*
- For works published prior to 1900, the place and date are sufficient.

Year of publication
- If no year of publication is given, write *n.d.* ("no date") in place of the date.
- If it is a multivolume edited work published over a period of more than one year, put the span of time as the year.

Sample citations for books and nonperiodical sources

1. Book by one author

In a note, the author's name is given in normal order.

> 1. Ezra Levant, *Ethical Oil: The Case for Canada's Oil Sands* (Toronto: McClelland and Stewart, 2010), 81.

In subsequent references, cite the author's last name only:

> 2. Levant, 81.

If the reference is to the same work as the reference before it, you can use the abbreviation *Ibid.*:

> 3. Ibid., 83.

In the bibliography, give the author's name in reverse order. For edited books, put *ed.* after the name.

> Graves, Roger, and Heather Graves, eds. *Writing Centres, Writing Seminars, Writing Culture: Teaching Writing in Anglo-Canadian Universities*. Winnipeg: Inkshed Publications, 2006.

2. Book by multiple authors

In a note, put all authors' names in normal order. For subsequent references, give only the authors' last names:

> 4. McClelland and Eismann, 32.

In the bibliography, give second and third authors' names in normal order.

> Linhout, Amanda, and Sara Corbett. *A House in the Sky: A Memoir*. New York: Scribner, 2013.

When there are more than three authors, give the name of the first author listed, followed by *et al.* in a note. However, in the bibliography, list all of the authors.

> 5. Jacqueline Jones et al., *Created Equal: A Social and Political History of the United States* (New York: Longman, 2003), 243.

3. **Book by a group or organization**
Note

> 6. KPMG Enterprise, *That'll Never Work: Business Lessons from Successful Canadian Entrepreneurs* (Toronto: Penguin Group, 2012), 111.

Bibliography

> KPMG Enterprise. *That'll Never Work: Business Lessons from Successful Canadian Entrepreneurs*. Toronto: Penguin Group, 2012.

4. **A selection in an anthology or a chapter in an edited collection**
Note

> 3. Robert Irish, "Forging the Teachable Moment: Developing Communication in and across an Engineering Curriculum," in *Writing Centres, Writing Seminars, Writing Culture: Teaching Writing in Anglo-Canadian Universities*, ed. Roger Graves and Heather Graves (Winnipeg: Inkshed Publications, 2006), 232.

Bibliography

Irish, Robert. "Forging the Teachable Moment: Developing Communication in and across an Engineering Curriculum." In *Writing Centres, Writing Seminars, Writing Culture: Teaching Writing in Anglo-Canadian Universities,* edited by Roger Graves and Heather Graves, 227–54. Winnipeg: Inkshed Publications, 2006.

5. Government document
Note

5. Health Canada Food Safety Assessment Program, *Assessment Report of the Canadian Food Inspection Agency Activities Related to the Safety of Aquaculture Products* (Ottawa: Minister of Public Works and Government Services Canada, 2001), 24.

Bibliography

Health Canada Food Safety Assessment Program. *Assessment Report of the Canadian Food Inspection Agency Activities Related to the Safety of Aquaculture Products.* Ottawa: Ministry of Public Works and Government Services, 2001.

6. Religious text

Citations from religious texts appear in the notes, but not in the bibliography. Give the version in parentheses in the first citation only.

Note

4. John 3:16 (King James Version).

16c Periodical Sources in CMS Style

Note

1. Marie Vander Kloet, "A Trip to the Co-op: The Production, Consumption and Salvation of Canadian Wilderness," *International Journal of Canadian Studies*, no. 39–40.

Bibliography

Vander Kloet, Marie. "A Trip to the Co-op: The Production, Consumption and Salvation of Canadian Wilderness." *International Journal of Canadian Studies*, no. 39–40 (2009): 231–51.

Author's or Editor's Name

- *Note:* The author's name is given in normal order.
- *Bibliography:* Give the author's last name first.

Title of Article

- Put the title in quotation marks. If there is a title of a book within the title, italicize it.
- Capitalize nouns, verbs, adjectives, adverbs, and pronouns, and the first word of the title and subtitle.

Publication Information

Name of journal

- Italicize the name of the journal.
- Journal titles are normally not abbreviated in the arts and humanities unless the title of the journal is an abbreviation (*PMLA, ELH*).

Volume, issue, and page numbers

- Place the volume number after the journal title without intervening punctuation.
- For journals that are paginated from issue to issue within a volume, you do not have to list the issue number.
- When a journal uses only issue numbers, not volumes, put a comma after the journal title.

Date

The year of publication, sometimes preceded by the exact date, month, or year, is given in parentheses after the volume number, or issue number, if provided.

Sample citations for periodical sources

7. Article by one author
Note

1. Kristen Welch, "Before and after the Tutorial: Writing Centers and Institutional Relationships," *Teaching English in the Two-Year College* 40 (2013): 425.

Bibliography

Welch, Kristen. "Before and after the Tutorial: Writing Centers and Institutional Relationships." *Teaching English in the Two-Year College* 40 (2013): 420–22.

8. Article by two or three authors
Note

2. Jo-Anne Andre and Roger Graves, "Writing Requirements across Nursing Programs in Canada," *Journal of Nursing Education* 52, no. 2 (February 2013): 93.

Bibliography

Andre, Jo-Anne, and Roger Graves. "Writing Requirements across Nursing Programs in Canada." *Journal of Nursing Education* 52, no. 2 (February 2013): 91–97.

9. Article by more than three authors
Note

5. Michael J. Thompson et al., "The Internal Rotation of the Sun," *Annual Review of Astronomy and Astrophysics* 41 (2003), 602.

Bibliography

Thompson, Michael J., Jorgen Christensen-Dalsgaard, Mark S. Miesch, and Juri Toomre. "The Internal Rotation of the Sun." *Annual Review of Astronomy and Astrophysics* 41 (2003): 599–643.

10. Journals paginated by volume

Note

7. Daniel Cole, "Writing Removal and Resistance: Native American Rhetoric in the Composition Classroom," *College Composition and Communication* 63 (2013): 128.

Bibliography

Cole, Daniel. "Writing Removal and Resistance: Native American Rhetoric in the Composition Classroom." *College Composition and Communication* 63 (2013): 122–44.

11. Journals paginated by issue

Note

5. Tzvetan Todorov, "The New World Disorder," *South Central Review* 19, no. 2 (2002): 29.

Bibliography

Todorov, Tzvetan. "The New World Disorder." *South Central Review* 19, no. 2 (2002): 28–32.

12. Weekly and biweekly magazines

Note

5. Michael Petrou, "Retribution the Canadian Way," *Maclean's*, March 19, 2012, 20.

Bibliography

Petrou, Michael. "Retribution the Canadian Way." *Maclean's*,
March 19, 2012, 20.

13. Newspaper article

Note

1. Andrew Coyne, "Canada at the Crossroads of Trade,"
National Post, March 18, 2012, sec. A.

Bibliography

Coyne, Andrew. "Canada at the Crossroads of Trade." *National
Post*, March 18, 2012, sec. A.

16d Online and Computer Sources in CMS Style

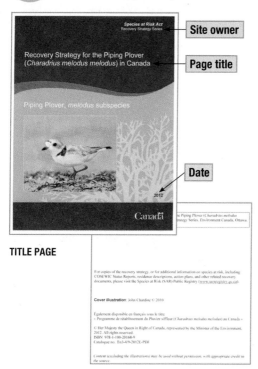

TITLE PAGE

14. Document or page from a website

To cite original content from within a website, include as many descriptive elements as you can: author of the page, title of the page, title and owner of the website, and the URL or DOI. Many journal articles or online books are given a digital object identifier (DOI), which provides a permanent link to the text. Include the date accessed only if no publication date is provided by the source or your instructor requires it. If you cannot locate an individual author, the owner of the site can stand in for the author.

Note

8. "Recovery Strategy for the Piping Plover (Charadrius melodus melodus) in Canada," *Environment Canada*, 2012, http://www .sararegistry.gc.ca/virtual_sara/files/plans/rs_piping_plover_melodus_ e1.pdf.

Bibliography

"Recovery Strategy for the Piping Plover (Charadrius melodus melodus) in Canada." *Ottawa: Environment Canada*, 2012.

15. Online book

Note

12. Angelina Grimké, *Appeal to the Christian Women of the South* (New York: New York Anti-Slavery Society, 1836), http:// utc.iath.virginia.edu/abolitn/abesaegat.html.

Bibliography

Grimké, Angelina. *Appeal to the Christian Women of the South.* Reprint of the 1836 New York Anti-Slavery Society edition, University of Virginia, 1998. http://utc.iath.virginia.edu /abolitn/abesaegat.html.

16. Online article

Note

13. Peter V. Hall and Amir J. Khan, "Differences in Hi-Tech Immigrant Earnings and Wages across Canadian Cities," *Canadian Geographer* 52 (2008): 271–90, doi:10.1111 /j.1541-0064.2008.00213.x.

Bibliography

Hall, Peter V., and Amir J. Khan. "Differences in Hi-Tech Immigrant Earnings and Wages across Canadian Cities." *Canadian Geographer* 52 (2008): 271–90. doi:10.1111/j.1541 -0064.2008.00213.x.

17. Documents and articles retrieved from database services

To cite documents or articles obtained through an Internet database, follow the CMS model for citing journal articles. Add the URL only if the database provides a stable one with the document. Otherwise, give the name of the database and put the document's identification number after it in parentheses, if one is provided.

Note

13. Susan Walker, "The Farmer in the Dell: At the Age of 85, Farmer Ed Burt Still Grows Most of What He Eats," *Toronto Star* (October 2014): IN5. *ProQuest.*

Bibliography

Walker, Susan. "The Farmer in the Dell: At the Age of 85, Farmer Ed Burt Still Grows Most of What He Eats." *Toronto Star* (October 2014): IN5. *ProQuest.*

18. Posting to a discussion list or group

To cite material from archived Internet forums, discussion groups, MOOs, or blogs, include the name of the post author, the name of the list or site, the date of the posting, and the URL. Limit your citation to notes or in-text citations.

Note

> 17. Janyce McGregor, "Not Up for Debate: The Throne Speech," *Inside Politics (blog)*, *CBC News*, June 3, 2011, http://www.cbc.ca/news/politics/inside-politics-blog/2011/06/throne-speech-debate-dont-hold-your-breath.html.

19. E-mail

Because personal e-mails are not available to the public, they are not usually listed in the bibliography.

> 11. Erik Lynn Williams, e-mail message to author, August 12, 2007.

20. Twitter

Note

> 4. Roger Graves, Twitter post, June 1, 2014, 10:24 am, https://twitter.com/rogergraves/status/473138136956940288.

Bibliography

> Graves, Roger. Twitter post. June 1, 2014, 10:24 am. https://twitter.com/rogergraves/status/473138136956940288.

21. Facebook

Note

> 12. "Globe and Mail Facebook Page," last modified June 9, 2014. Accessed June 9, 2014.

Bibliography

> "Globe and Mail Facebook Page." Last modified June 9, 2014. Accessed June 9, 2014.

Sample Research Paper and References

1

Elizabeth Moore

British History and Literature 102

April 24, 2014

Love and Marriage in the Works and Lives
of Elizabeth Cary and Lady Mary Wroth

The work of Elizabeth Cary, titled Lady Falkland,
and Lady Mary Wroth looks with a critical eye at the
coupling of love and marriage. For early modern women,
reality often composed itself in the form of marriage
and love of something unrelated to one's husband.
Forced to eke out a place in their prescribed roles as
wife and mother for their own intellectual expression,
Cary and Wroth wrote stories about women who found
themselves caught between their own powerful desires
and the men who controlled their lives. Their writing is
important today not only as literature but as an
invaluable record of the thoughts and self-expression
of women in a time when their lives were not their
own. The protagonists of Cary's and Wroth's work
explore the meaning of love and marriage, both topics
complex and often dissatisfying in the context of their
time. Like their fictional characters, Cary and Wroth
navigated the rocky terrain of the heart and the mind.

> Double-space
> all of your paper,
> including end
> notes and the
> bibliography.

---

*Portions shown in this paper are adjusted to fit the space limitations of this book. Follow the actual
dimensions discussed in this book and your instructor's directions."

2

Their biographies both inform and contradict their writing. The dialogue between their realities and their fiction considers what it meant to be woman in the early modern period.

Elizabeth Cary and Mary Wroth were born Elizabeth Tanfield and Mary Sidney, respectively. They were both eminently well educated in childhood. Tanfield, born in 1585, had taught herself "French, Spanish, Italian, Latin, Hebrew and 'Transylvanian'" by the age of 4 and successfully argued for the acquittal of a woman accused of witchcraft at 10.[1] Sidney, born in 1587, was the niece of noted Renaissance poet and literary patron Mary Herbert, countess of Pembroke, for whom she was named. She spent part of her childhood in extended visits with her aunt. She was active in the court of King James I and VI and performed in several masques.[2] Both Sidney and Tanfield were brought up in academically fertile environments. . . .

Use superscript numbers to indicate foot or end notes. Include details of publication information in the note. Number notes consecutively throughout your paper.

3

Notes

1. Nancy Cotton Pearse, "Elizabeth Cary, Renaissance Playwright," *Texas Studies in Literature and Language* 18 (1977): 603.

2. Josephine Roberts, "The Biographical Problem of *Pamphilia to Amphilanthus,*" *Tulsa Studies in Women's Literature* 1, no. 1 (1982): 48. http://www.jstor.org/stable/464091.

Notes are numbered in the order they appear in your paper. Bibliographic entries are listed in alphabetical order.

4

Bibliography

Pearse, Nancy Cotton. "Elizabeth Cary, Renaissance Playwright." *Texas Studies in Literature and Language* 18 (1977): 601–8.

Roberts, Josephine. "The Biographical Problem of *Pamphilia to Amphilanthus.*" *Tulsa Studies in Women's Literature* 1, no. 1 (1982): 43–53. http://www.jstor.org/stable/464091.

17 | CSE Documentation

QUICK*TAKE*

- Cite books in CSE-style references (see pp. 160–162)
- Cite articles and online sources in CSE-style references (see pp. 163–166)

The Council of Science Editors publishes *Scientific Style and Format: The CSE Manual for Authors, Editors, and Publishers*, currently in its eighth edition (2014). The *CSE Manual* is widely followed by writers in the natural sciences.

The preferred documentation system in CSE places references in the body of the text marked by a superscript number that immediately follows punctuation. For example,

Cold fingers and toes are common circulatory problems found in most heavy cigarette smokers.[1]

This number corresponds to a numbered entry on the alphabetized CSE source list, titled *References*. To create a CSE references page, follow these guidelines:

1. Title your page "References," and centre this title at the top of the page.
2. Single-space within citations and double-space between citations.
3. For papers using the **citation-name system**, list and number citations in alphabetical order. Begin each citation with its citation number, followed by a period, flush left.
4. List authors by last name, followed by initials. Capitalize only first words and proper nouns in cited titles. Titles are not underlined, and articles are not placed in quotations. Names of journals should be abbreviated where possible.
5. Cite publication year, and volume or page numbers if applicable.

17a In-Text Citations in CSE Style

CSE documentation of sources does not require the names of authors in the text, only a number that refers to the references at the end.

> In 2006, a Gallup International poll found that 26% of individuals around the world see poverty as humanity's most pressing problem.[1]

The superscript [1] refers to the first entry in the references, where readers will find a complete citation for this source.

What if you need more than one citation in a passage?

If the numbers are consecutive, separate with a hyphen or an en dash. If non-consecutive, use a comma without a space.

> These films tend to form multilayers and are relatively disordered.[1,3,7-9]

17b Books and Nonperiodical Sources in CSE-Style References

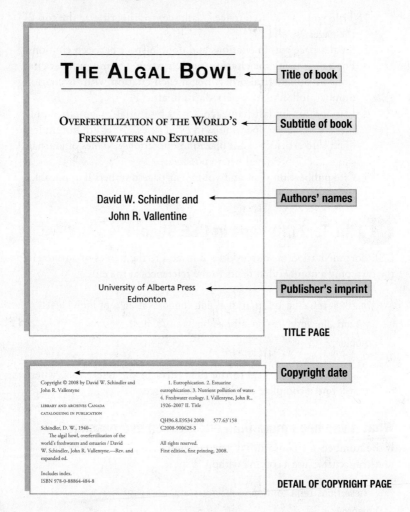

THE ALGAL BOWL ← Title of book

OVERFERTILIZATION OF THE WORLD'S ← Subtitle of book
FRESHWATERS AND ESTUARIES

David W. Schindler and ← Authors' names
John R. Vallentine

University of Alberta Press ← Publisher's imprint
Edmonton

TITLE PAGE

Copyright © 2008 by David W. Schindler and ← Copyright date
John R. Vallentyne

LIBRARY AND ARCHIVES CANADA
CATALOGUING IN PUBLICATION

Schindler, D. W., 1940–
The algal howl, overfertilization of the
world's freshwaters and estuaries / David
W. Schindler, John R. Vallentyne.—Rev. and
expanded ed.

Includes index.
ISBN 978-0-88864-484-8

1. Eutrophication. 2. Estuarine
eutrophication. 3. Nutrient pollution of water.
4. Freshwater ecology. I. Vallentyne, John R.,
1926–2007 II. Title

QH96.8.E9S34 2008   577.63'158
C2008-900628-3

All rights reserved.
First edition, first printing, 2008.

DETAIL OF COPYRIGHT PAGE

1. Schindler DW, Vallentine JR. The algal bowl: overfertilization of the world's freshwaters and estuaries. Edmonton (AB): University of Alberta Press; 2008. 348 p.

Author's or Editor's Name

The author's last name comes first, followed by the initials of the author's first name and middle name (if provided). If an editor, put the word *editor* after the name.

Book Title

- Do not italicize or underline titles.
- Capitalize only the first word and proper nouns.

Publication Information

Year of publication

- The year comes after the other publication information. It follows a semicolon.
- If it is a multivolume edited work, published over a period of more than one year, give the span of years.

Page numbers

- When citing an entire book, give the total number of pages: *348 p.*
- When citing part of a book, give the page range for the selection: *p. 60–90.*

Sample references for books and nonperiodical sources in CSE style

1. **Book by one author/editor**

   2. Lay DC. Linear algebra and its applications. Boston (MA): Pearson; 2006. 492 p.

2. **Book by two or more authors/editors**

   3. O'Day DH, Horgen PA, editors. Sexual interactions in eukaryotic microbes. New York (NY): Academic; 1981. 407 p.

3. Book by a group or organization

> 4. Biological Survey of Canada. Insects of the Yukon. Ottawa (ON): BSC; 1997. 1034 p.

4. A selection in an anthology or a chapter in an edited collection

The author of the selection is listed first. The year given is for the collection. Put the word *In* and a colon before the editor of the collection.

> 7. Kraft K, Baines DM. Computer classrooms and third grade development. In: Green MD, editor. Computers and early development. New York (NY): Academic; 1997. p. 168–79.

5. Technical and research reports

> 8. Austin A, Baldwin R, editors. Faculty collaboration: enhancing the quality of scholarship and teaching. ASCHE-ERIC Higher Education Report 7. Washington (DC): George Washington University; 1991.

17c Periodical Sources in CSE-Style References

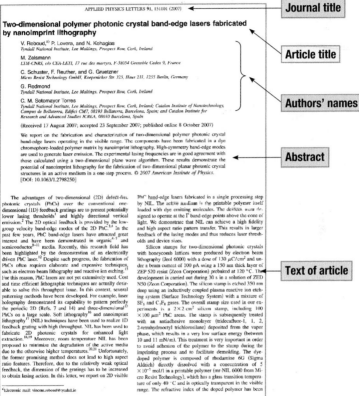

Journal title → APPLIED PHYSICS LETTERS 91, 151101 (2007)

Article title → Two-dimensional polymer photonic crystal band-edge lasers fabricated by nanoimprint lithography

Authors' names

V. Reboud,[a] P. Lovera, and N. Kehagias
Tyndall National Institute, Lee Maltings, Prospect Row, Cork, Ireland

M. Zelsmann
LTM-CNRS, c/o CEA-LETI, 17 rue des martyrs, F-38054 Grenoble Cedex 9, France

C. Schuster, F. Reuther, and G. Gruetzner
Micro Resist Technology GmbH, Koepenicker Str 325, Haus 211, 1255 Berlin, Germany

G. Redmond
Tyndall National Institute, Lee Maltings, Prospect Row, Cork, Ireland

C. M. Sotomayor Torres
Tyndall National Institute, Lee Maltings, Prospect Row, Cork, Ireland; Catalan Institute of Nanotechnology, Campus de Bellaterra, Edifici CM7, 08193 Bellaterra, Barcelona, Spain; and Catalan Institute for Research and Advanced Studies ICREA, 08010 Barcelona, Spain

(Received 17 August 2007; accepted 23 September 2007; published online 8 October 2007)

Abstract → We report on the fabrication and characterization of two-dimensional polymer photonic crystal band-edge lasers operating in the visible range. The components have been fabricated in a dye chromophore-loaded polymer matrix by nanoimprint lithography. High-symmetry band-edge modes are used to generate laser emission. The experimental lasing frequencies are in good agreement with those calculated using a two-dimensional plane wave algorithm. These results demonstrate the potential of nanoimprint lithography for the fabrication of two-dimensional planar photonic crystal structures in an active medium in a one step process. © 2007 American Institute of Physics.
[DOI: 10.1063/1.2798250]

Text of article

The advantages of two-dimensional (2D) defect-free photonic crystals (PhCs) over the conventional one-dimensional (1D) feedback gratings are to present potentially lower lasing thresholds[1] and highly directional vertical emission.[2] The 2D optical feedback is provided by the low-group velocity band-edge modes of the 2D PhC.[3,4] In the past few years, PhC band-edge lasers have attracted great interest and have been demonstrated in organic[4-7] and semiconductor[8-11] media. Recently, this research field has been highlighted by the demonstration of an electrically driven PhC laser.[12] Despite such progress, the fabrication of PhCs often requires elaborate and expensive techniques, such as electron-beam lithography and reactive ion etching.[13] For this reason, PhC lasers are not yet extensively used. Cost and time efficient lithographic techniques are actually desirable to solve this throughput issue. In this context, several patterning methods have been developed. For example, laser holography demonstrated its capability to pattern perfectly the periodic 2D (Refs. 7 and 14) and three-dimensional[15] PhCs on a large scale. Soft lithography[16] and nanoimprint lithography[17] (NIL) techniques have been used to realize 1D feedback grating with high throughput. NIL has been used to fabricate 2D photonic crystals for enhanced light extraction.[18,19] Moreover, room temperature NIL has been proposed to minimize the degradation of the active media due to the otherwise higher temperatures.[20,21] Unfortunately, the former promising method does not lead to high aspect ratio features. Therefore, due to the relatively weak optical feedback, the dimension of the gratings has to be increased to obtain lasing action. In this letter, we report on 2D visible

PhC band-edge lasers fabricated in a single processing step by NIL. The active medium is the printable polymer itself loaded with dye emitting molecules. The devices were designed to operate at the Γ band-edge points above the cone of light. We demonstrate that NIL can achieve a high fidelity and high aspect ratio pattern transfer. This results in larger feedback of the lasing modes and thus reduces laser thresholds and device sizes.

Silicon stamps for two-dimensional photonic crystals with honeycomb lattices were produced by electron beam lithography (Jeol 6000) with a dose of 130 μC/cm² and under a beam current of 100 pA using a 150 nm thick layer of ZEP 520 resist (Zeon Corporation) prebaked at 120 °C. The development is carried out during 30 s in a solution of ZED N50 (Zeon Corporation). The silicon stamp is etched 350 nm deep using an inductively coupled plasma reactive ion etching system (Surface Technology System) with a mixture of SF_6 and C_4F_8 gases. The overall stamp size used in our experiments is a 2×2 cm² silicon stamp, including 100 $\times 100$ μm² PhC areas. The stamp is subsequently treated with an antiadhesive monolayer (tridecafluor-1, 1, 2, 2-tetrahydrooctyl trichlorosilane) deposited from the vapor phase, which results in a very low surface energy (between 10 and 11 mN/m). This treatment is very important in order to avoid adhesion of the polymer to the stamp during the imprinting process and to facilitate demolding. The dye-doped polymer is composed of rhodamine 6G (Sigma Aldrich) directly dissolved with a concentration of 5 $\times 10^{-3}$ mol/l in a printable polymer (mr-NIL 6000 from Micro Resist Technology), which has a glass transition temperature of only 40 °C and is optically transparent in the visible range. The refractive index of the doped polymer has been

[a]Electronic mail: vincent.reboud@tyndall.ie

1. Reboud V, Lovera P, Kehagias N, Zelsmann M, Schuster C, Reuther F, Gruetzner G, Redmond G, Sotomayor Torres CM. Two-dimensional polymer photonic crystal band-edge lasers fabricated by nanoimprint lithography. Appl Physics Let 91, 151101 2007.

Author's Name

The author's last name comes first, followed by the initials of the author's first name and middle name (if provided). For up to ten authors, list them last name first, followed by the initials, in the order listed on the article. If there are more than ten authors, list the first author and initials, followed by *et al*.

Publication Information

Name of journal
• Journal titles can be abbreviated.
• Capitalize the journal title.

Date of publication, volume, and issue numbers
For continuously paginated journals, include only the year and volume number, not the issue number.

Title of Article ◄

• Do not italicize or underline titles.
• Capitalize only the first word and proper nouns.

Sample references for periodical sources in CSE style

6. Article by one author

1. Nielsen TVJ. Influence of prey distribution and salinity stress on the geographic distribution of the marine snail Lirabuccinum dirum. J Exp Mar Biol Ecol. 2011;410:80-86.

7. Article by two or more authors/editors

> 2. Almeda R, Messmer KM, Sampedro N, Gosselin LA. Feeding rates and abundance of marine invertebrate planktonic larvae under harmful algal bloom conditions off Vancouver Island. Harmful Algae. 2011;10:194-206.

8. Article by a group or organization

> 3. Centre for Science in the Public Interest. The real cost of red meat. Nutrition Action Health Letter 2009;36(5):1+.

9. Article with no identifiable author

Alphabetize the article by title.

10. Journals paginated by issue

Use the month or season of publication (and day, if given) for journals that have no volume or issue number.

> 8. Solar-Tuttle R. The invincible ones. Harv AIDS Rev. 2000 Spring-Summer: 19-20.

17d Unpublished Sources

11. Interviews

Insert a parenthetical reference in the text—"(interview)"—to cite an interview with a person if the interview has not been published. Do not include an entry in the References for any unpublished material, including an unpublished interview.

Online Sources in CSE-Style References

12. Online journal articles

1. Schunck CH, Shin Y, Schirotzek A, Zwierlein MW, Ketterle A. Pairing without superfluidity: the ground state of an imbalanced fermi mixture. Science [Internet]. 2007 [cited 2007 June 15]; 316(5826):867-870. Available from: http://www.sciencemag.org/cgi/content/full/3165826/867/DC1

13. Scientific databases on the Internet

3. Comprehensive Large Array-data Steward System [Internet]. 2007. Release 4.2. Silver Spring (MD): National Environmental Satellite, Data, and Information Service (US). [updated 2007 May 2; cited 2007 May 14]. Available from: http://www.class.noaa.gov/saa/products/welcome

14. Print documents accessed on the Internet

4. Fahnestock J. Rhetorical figures in science [electronic resource]. 1999. New York (NY): Oxford University Press. 234 p. [cited 2011 May 2]. Available from: http://lib.myilibrary.com.login.ezproxy.library.ualberta.ca/Open.aspx?id=76157&loc=&srch=undefined&src=0

18 | IEEE Documentation

QUICK*TAKE*

* Cite books in IEEE-style references (see p. 171)
* Cite articles (see pp. 169–170) and online sources in IEEE-style references (see pp. 172–173)

The Institute of Electrical and Electronic Engineers (IEEE) publishes the *IEEE Editorial Style Manual* to provide editorial guidelines for IEEE transactions, journals, and letters. For additional information on how to format citations and references using IEEE documentation, search "citation reference" at http://www.ieee.org

IEEE documentation style uses citations in the body of the document to identify immediately sources of information and a list of references at the end of the document that provides complete and detailed information for all the sources cited.

Citations

IEEE documentation style encloses citation numbers in the text of the paper in square brackets—for example, [1]. All additional bibliographical information about the citation appears in the list of references at the end of the document. Place citation numbers directly after the reference. Punctuate outside the square bracket, and use commas to separate multiple references (for example, [2], [7], [17].).

Citation-name substitution

IEEE style suggests substituting reference list numbers for the name of the author(s) where appropriate. For example, if you want to attribute a finding to a research group, substitute the number of the reference for the list of authors' names. In contrast, if you want to attribute something like a theory to the person who developed it, use the author's name.

List of references

Your list of references should include all the sources that you used in writing the document.

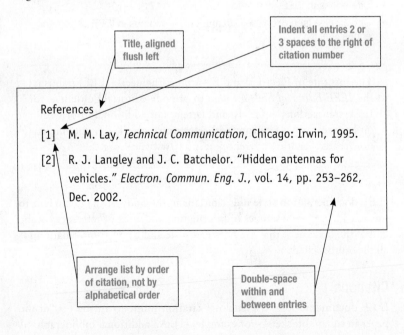

Title, aligned flush left

Indent all entries 2 or 3 spaces to the right of citation number

References

[1]   M. M. Lay, *Technical Communication*, Chicago: Irwin, 1995.

[2]   R. J. Langley and J. C. Batchelor. "Hidden antennas for vehicles." *Electron. Commun. Eng. J.*, vol. 14, pp. 253–262, Dec. 2002.

Arrange list by order of citation, not by alphabetical order

Double-space within and between entries

18a Periodical Sources

APPLIED THEORY

▼ SUMMARY
- Explores the claim that current internationalization and localization efforts presume particular cultural rather than structural or architectural reconsideration
- Maps cultural dimensions to different elements of information architecture

Information Architecture:
Intercultural Human Factors

MATTHEW MCCOOL

INTRODUCTION

During the past nine years I have developed a variety of online products for domestic and international audiences, ranging from the simple to the complex, for both public and private sectors. During this time the most difficult projects I worked on were not how to modify Java APIs or customize complex applications, but rather making basic information available to international and intercultural audiences. Although I teamed with reputable localization personnel from Germany, Japan, France, and Spain to make our online documentation accessible for these respective audiences, the result was generally disappointing. In nearly every case something seemed to go wrong, a conclusion based on the excessive number of call center questions from our international customers.

We arrived at this realization when comparing not only previous product support calls from these same customers but also in comparing these calls with those from our domestic audience. From our perspective, nothing was considerably different. We accounted for time, currency, and color. The translations were rhetorical and not literal, ensuring linguistic transference from English to the target language. And these customers were also very important, comprising the bulk of total revenue, a fact that justified the enormous time and expense of our localization efforts. Everything else was the same—the same content, the same information superstructure, the same chunking and navigation.

We were mystified as to how our international deliverables, especially for Japan, were failing so much more than the domestic equivalent. In the end the problem was never solved, the companies I worked for endured turbulent times, and I moved on to other equally interesting projects. It was several years later when I learned about cultural dimensions, and so I began to wonder whether the absence of these core values in our design may have caused our troubles.

Traditionally, the process of making online information accessible to different cultures amounted to basic adaptations of time, currency, and color (Hoft 1995). Trans-

lation, although never a direct transmission from one language to the next (Kaplan 1966; Connor 1996), incorporated few if any rhetorical considerations. Despite earnest efforts to design for a rather different audience, albeit internationalization or localization, numerous cultural adaptations failed to be considered.

Excellent research has been conducted about both information architecture and intercultural communication, but until recently, they rarely found cause for convergence. For example, in the May 2000 *Technical communication* special section on information design, none of the articles specifically address the coalescence of superstructures, chunking, and navigation for the online environment. Similarly, although excellent articles have been published regarding online media and cultural values (for example, Fukuoka and colleagues 1999; Arnold 2000; Qiaye 2000), touching on core cultural dimensions, none have addressed their convergence with and effect on information architecture.

While authors in these two areas have focused on specific or exclusive problems, they have never been meaningfully considered or studied together. If internationalization and localization processes are to be useful and effective, overlaying cultural dimensions on information structures may prove to be the final variable toward effective online localization.

The process of overlaying cultural dimensions on information architecture is a new approach toward internationalization and localization. Much good and useful work has been done with regard to culture and online information, but rarely have these explorations incorporated the deeper currents of culture. This fact is unfortunate because core cultural values, those dimensions which influence how we perceive and ascribe meaning to the world (Kaplan 1966; Victor 1992; Connor 1996; Hofstede 1997; Trompenaars 1998), are possibly the most important factors

Manuscript received 27 February 2005; revised 3 December 2005; accepted 5 December 2005.

1. Article by one author

[1] M. McCool, "Information architecture: Intercultural human factors," *Tech. Commun.*, vol. 53, no. 2, pp. 167–183, May 2006.

Author's Name
Use author's initials, then surname, followed by a comma.

Title of Article
- Put the title in quotation marks.
- Capitalize first word of title and subtitle.

Publication Information

Name of journal
- Italicize and abbreviate the name of the journal.
- Abbreviate journal titles, as appropriate.

Volume, issue, and page numbers
- Abbreviate the words "volume" and "number," as shown, separated by a comma.
- Include page numbers, formatted as shown.
- Include the abbreviated month and the year of the journal issue.

Date
Date is included with month at the end of the citation.

2. Article by two or more authors

[9] Anne Parker and Aidan Topping, "Designing rubrics for communication courses in Engineering: A work in progress," *Proc. CEEA Canadian Engineering Education Conf.*, CEEA13; *Paper 143* (Montreal, QC; 17-20 June 2013), 6 pp., 2013.

3. Article by a group or organization

[3] Centre for Science in the Public Interest, "Behind the label," *Nutrition Action Healthletter*, vol. 34, no. 7, p. 11, Sept. 2007.

18b Books

4. Book by a single author/editor

> [5]   D. Roam, *The Back of the Napkin: Solving Problems and Selling Ideas with Pictures*. New York: Portfolio, 2010.

5. Book by two or more authors/editors

> [1]   C. Heath and D. Heath, *Made to Stick: Why Some Ideas Survive and Others Die*. New York: Random House, 2007.

6. Book by a group or organization

> [3]   World Health Organization, *Advancing Safe Motherhood Through Human Rights*. Geneva, Switzerland: World Health Organization, 2001.

18c Reports

7. Report by a single author

> [4]   C. Rudin-Brown, "Strategies for reducing drive distraction from in-vehicle telematics devices: Report on industry and public consultations," Road Safety and Motor Vehicle Regulation Directorate, Ottawa, ON, TP 14409 E, 2005.

8. Report by an organization

> [3]   Health Canada Food Safety Assessment Program, "Assessment reports of the Canadian Food Inspection Agency activities related to the safety of aquaculture products," Ministry of Public Works and Government Services, Ottawa, ON, Cat. H39-577/2001E, 2001.

18d Online Sources in IEEE Style

Site owner

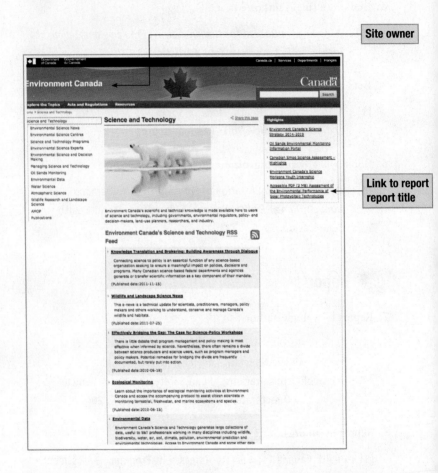

Site owner

Link to report
report title

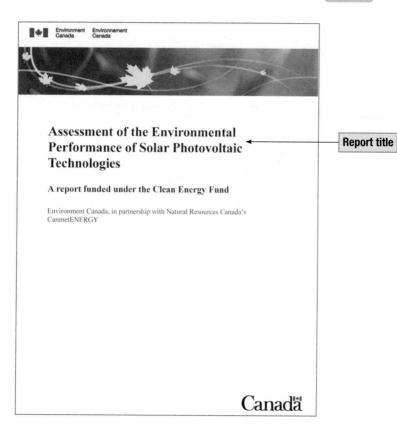

Assessment of the Environmental
Performance of Solar Photovoltaic   ← Report title
Technologies

A report funded under the Clean Energy Fund

Environment Canada, in partnership with Natural Resources Canada's
CanmetENERGY

Canada

9. **Documents from a website**

Online Report

[7] Environment Canada. (2012). "Assessment of the
     environmental performance of solar photovoltaic
     technologies." Environment Canada. Ottawa, ON. [Online].
     Available: http://www.ec.gc.ca/scitech/B53B14DE
     -034C-457B-8B2B-39AFCFED04E.pdf.

Online Article

[3] P. Agre. (1998, Mar.). "The Internet and public discourse."
First Monday [Online]. 3 (3). Available: http://www.firstmonday
.dk/issues/issue3_3/agre/.

PART 4 Style and Language

19 | Writing with Power

QUICKTAKE

- Make your writing active (see below)
- Use agents in your writing (see p. 178)
- Vary your sentences (see p. 179)

Keeping a few principles in mind can make your writing a pleasure to read instead of a chore.

In photographs
You imagine actions when subjects are captured in motion.

In writing
Readers expect you to express action in verbs:
fly, rip, freeride, jump, lay down, charge.

In photographs
Viewers interpret the most prominent person or thing as the subject—what the visual is about.

In writing
Readers interpret the first person or thing they meet in a sentence as what the sentence is about (the snowboarder, the snowboard). They expect that person or thing to do the action expressed in the verb.

19a **Recognize Active and Passive Voice**

In the **active voice** the subject of the sentence is the actor. In the **passive voice** the subject is being acted upon.

Active   After each exposure we collected a new image, and we calculated the distribution of the photon counts.

Passive   After each exposure a new image was collected, and the distribution of the photon counts was calculated.

Disciplines in humanities, arts, and some social sciences favour the active voice because it adds impact to writing. Observe the difference:

Passive   Empirical work using critical methodologies will now be accepted by editors.

Active   Editors now accept empirical work using critical methodologies.

In contrast, disciplines such as science use the passive voice to emphasize the objects of study over the actors. In the following example, the actions matter more than the actors:

Passive   The woman thought to be the model for Leonardo da Vinci's Mona Lisa is being exhumed to determine whether her facial structure matches that depicted in the painting.

Many writers in science overuse the passive voice, making their writing a chore to read. When writing for science and social science disciplines, use the active voice as often as possible to keep your reader interested.

19b **Use Action Verbs**

Where are the action words in the following paragraph?

Red hair flying, professional snowboarder and skateboarder Shaun White is a two-time Olympic gold medalist with a record score of 48.4 at the 2010 Winter Olympics. White was a skier before he was five, but became a snowboarder at age six, and by age seven he was a professional, receiving corporate sponsorships. At age nine,

White became friends with professional skateboarder Tony
Hawk, who was White's mentor in becoming a professional skateboarder. White is known for accomplishing several "firsts" in snowboarding, including being the first to land back-to-back double
corks and to master a trick called a "Cab 7 Melon Grab." He is also
the holder of record for the highest score in the men's halfpipe at
the Winter Olympics.

No action words here! The passage describes a series of actions, yet the only
verbs are forms of *be (was, were)*, and many actions are hidden in nouns.
Think about what the actions are and choose powerful verbs that express
those actions.

Red hair flying, professional snowboarder and skateboarder Shaun
White scored a 48.4 during the 2010 Winter Olympics and won his
second gold medal. White skied before he was five, but switched
to snowboarding at age six, and by age seven received corporate
sponsorships. At age nine, White befriended professional skateboarder Tony Hawk, who mentored White and helped him become
a professional skateboarder. White has accomplished several
"firsts" in snowboarding, including landing back-to-back double
corks and mastering a trick called a "Cab 7 Melon Grab." He also
holds the record for the highest score in the men's halfpipe at the
Winter Olympics.

Much academic writing uses nouns rather than verbs to express action. Once nouns are changed into verbs, the writing becomes clearer and
more dynamic.

The arson unit ~~conducted an investigation of~~ investigated the mys-
terious fire.

The committee ~~had a debate over~~ debated how best to spend the
surplus funds.

Notice that changing nouns into verbs also eliminates unnecessary words.

19c Name Your Agents

The **agent** is the person or thing that does the action. Powerful writing
puts the agents in sentences.

Focus on people

Read the following sentence aloud:

> Utilization of a MIDI keyboard for digital song performance capture on the laptop will enable easier subsequent uploading to the website.

It sounds lifeless, doesn't it? Putting people into the sentence makes it come alive:

> If we play the song on a MIDI keyboard, we can capture the digitized sound on our laptop and more easily upload it to our website.

Including people makes your writing more emphatic. Most readers relate better to people than to abstractions. Putting people in your sentences also introduces active verbs because people do things.

Focus on your agents

Even when you are not writing about people, keep the focus on your agents. Read this short section from a report written by an engineer who was asked to recommend which of two types of valves an oil company should purchase for one of its refineries.

> Although the two systems function similarly, Farval valves have two distinct advantages. First, Farval grease valves include a pin indicator that shows whether the valve is working. Alemite valves must be checked by taking them apart. Second, Farval valves have metal seals, while Alemite valves have rubber grommet seals. If an Alemite valve fails, the pressure will force grease past the rubber grommet seals, creating a grease puddle on the floor. By contrast, Farval's metal seals contain the grease if the valve fails.

This engineer not only makes a definite recommendation supported by reasons, she also makes her report easy to read by keeping the focus on the two types of valves she is comparing.

 Vary Your Sentences

Read the following passage.

> On the first day Garth, Jim, and I paddled fourteen miles down Johnstone Strait. We headed down the strait about five more miles

to Robson Bight. It is a famous scratching place for orcas. The Bight is a small bay. We paddled out into the strait so we could see the entire Bight. There were no orcas inside. By this time we were getting tired. We were hungry. The clouds assumed a wintry dark thickness. The wind was kicking up against us. Our heads were down going into the cold spray.

The subject matter is interesting, but the writing isn't. The passage is a series of short sentences, one after the other. When you have too many short sentences in a row, try combining a few of them.

The result of combining some (but not all) short sentences is a paragraph whose sentences match the interest of the subject.

On the first day Garth, Jim, and I paddled fourteen miles down Johnstone Strait. We headed down the strait about five more miles to Robson Bight, a small bay known as a famous scratching place for orcas. We paddled out into the strait so we could see the entire Bight, but there were no orcas inside. By this time we were tired and hungry, the clouds had assumed a wintry dark thickness, and the wind was kicking up against us—our heads dropped going into the cold spray.

20 | Writing Concisely

QUICK*TAKE*

- Eliminate unnecessary words (see p. 181)
- Reduce wordy phrases (see p. 181)
- Simplify tangled sentences (see p. 183)

Clutter creeps into our lives every day. Clutter also creeps into writing through unnecessary words, inflated constructions, and excessive jargon.

20a Eliminate Unnecessary Words

In regards to the website, the content is pretty successful in consideration of the topic. The site is fairly good writing-wise and is very unique in telling you how to adjust the rear derailleur one step at a time.

The words in orange are clutter. Get rid of the clutter. You can say the same thing with half the words and gain more impact as a result.

The well-written website on bicycle repair provides step-by-step instructions on adjusting your rear derailleur.

Redundancy

Some words act as modifiers, but all they do is repeat the meaning of the word they pretend to modify. Have you heard someone refer to a *personal friend*? Aren't all friends personal? Likewise, you may have heard expressions such as *red in colour, small in size, round in shape*, or *honest truth*. Imagine *red* not referring to colour or *round* not referring to shape.

 20b Reduce Wordy Phrases

Many inexperienced writers use phrases like "It is my opinion that" or "I think that" to begin sentences. These phrases are deadly to read. If you find them in your prose, cut them. Unless a writer is citing a source, we assume that the ideas are the writer's.

Some coaches are among the worst at using many words for what could be said in a few:

After much deliberation about Chevalier's future in hockey with regard to possible permanent head injuries, I came to the conclusion that it would be in his best interest not to continue his pursuit of playing hockey again.

The coach might have said simply:

Because Chevalier risks permanent injury if he plays hockey again, I decided to release him from the team.

Speakers and writers who impress us are those who use words efficiently.

COMMON ERRORS

Empty intensifiers

Intensifiers modify verbs, adjectives, and other adverbs, and they often are overused. One of the most overused intensifiers is *very*. Take the following sentence as an example:

> The new copper roof was **very bright** on a sunny day.

New copper reflects almost all light. *Very bright* isn't a revealing description. Thus another adjective would be more descriptive:

> The new copper roof was **blinding** on a sunny day.

Very and *totally* are but two of a list of empty intensifiers that usually can be eliminated with no loss of meaning. Other empty intensifiers include *absolutely, awfully, definitely, incredibly, particularly,* and *really*.

Remember: When you use *very, totally*, or another intensifier before an adjective or adverb, always ask yourself whether there is a more accurate adjective or adverb you could use to express the same thought.

Wordy phrases

Certain stock phrases plague writing in the workplace, in the media, and in academia. Many can be replaced by one or two words with no loss in meaning.

Wordy	Concise
at this point in time	now
due to the fact that	because
for the purpose of	for
have the ability to	can
in order to	to
in spite of the fact that	although
in the event that	if
met with her approval	she approved

20c Simplify Tangled Sentences

Long sentences can be graceful and forceful. Such sentences, however, often require several revisions before they achieve elegance. Too often long sentences reflect wandering thoughts that the writer did not bother to go back and sort out. Two of the most important strategies for untangling long sentences are described in Section 19b on using action verbs and in Section 19c on naming your agents. Here are some other strategies.

Revise expletives

Expletives are empty words that can occupy the subject position in a sentence. The most frequently used expletives are *there is*, *there are*, and *it is*.

| Wordy | There were several important differences between the rock samples that we collected from the canyon walls. |

To simplify the sentence, find the agent and make it the subject.

| Revised | The rock samples that we collected from the canyon walls differed significantly. |

A few kinds of sentences—for example, *It is raining*—do require you to use an expletive. In most cases, however, expletives add unnecessary words, and sentences usually read better without them.

Use positive constructions

Sentences become wordy and hard to read if they include two or more negatives such as the words *no*, *not*, and *nor*, and the prefixes *un-* and *mis-*. For example:

| Difficult | A not uncommon complaint among employers of new graduates is that they cannot communicate effectively in writing. |

| Revised | Employers frequently complain that new graduates cannot write effectively. |

| Even Simpler | Employers value the rare graduate who can write well. |

Phrasing sentences positively usually makes them more economical. Moreover, it makes your style more forceful and direct.

Simplify sentence structure

Long sentences can be hard to read, not because they are long but because they are convoluted and hide the relationships among ideas. Take the following sentence as an example.

> Some historians are arguing that World War II actually ended with German reunification in 1990 instead of when the Japanese surrendered in 1945, after which time the Cold War got in the way of formal legal settlements among the involved nations and Germany was divided between the Western powers and the Soviet Union meaning that no comprehensive peace treaty was signed.

This sentence is hard to read. To rewrite sentences like this one, find the main ideas, then determine the relationships among them.

After examining the sentence, you decide there are two key ideas:

1 Some historians argue that World War II actually ended in 1990 with German reunification, not when the Japanese surrendered in 1945.

2 The Cold War and the division of Germany between the Western powers and the Soviet Union hindered formal legal settlements among the involved nations.

Next ask what the relationship is between the two ideas. When you identify the key ideas, the relationship is often obvious; in this case (2) is the cause of (1). Thus the word you want to connect the two ideas is *because*.

> Because the Cold War and the division of Germany between the Western powers and the Soviet Union hindered formal legal settlements among the involved nations, some historians argue that World War II actually ended in 1990 with German reunification rather than with the Japanese surrender in 1945.

The revised sentence is both clearer and more concise, reducing the number of words from forty-two to twenty-five.

21 | Writing with Emphasis

QUICKTAKE

- Manage emphasis in your sentences (see p. 186)
- Use parallelism correctly (see p. 189)

Photographs and writing gain energy when you emphasize key ideas.

In visuals

Photographers create emphasis by composing an image to direct the attention of the viewer. Putting people and objects in the foreground and making them stand out against the background gives them emphasis.

In writing

You have many tools for creating emphasis. You can design a page to gain emphasis by using headings, white space, type size, colour, and boldfacing. Equally important, learning the craft of structuring sentences will empower you to give your writing emphasis.

21a Manage Emphasis Within Sentences

Put your main ideas in main clauses

Placing more important information in main clauses and less important information in subordinate clauses emphasizes what is important.

In the following paragraph all the sentences are main clauses:

> More Canadians are taking herbal remedies. They think that natural herbs must be safe. The remedies can cause bad reactions. They can blunt the effectiveness of prescription drugs. They can also interact with other health products.

This paragraph is grammatically correct, but it does not help the reader understand which pieces of information the author wants to emphasize. Combining the simple sentences into main and subordinate clauses and phrases can significantly improve the paragraph.

First, identify the main ideas:

> More Canadians are taking herbal remedies. They think that natural herbs are safe.

These ideas can be combined into one sentence:

> More Canadians are taking herbal remedies because they think they are safe.

Now think about the relationship of the three remaining sentences to the main ideas. Those sentences explain the contrasting view; thus the relationship is *but*.

> More Canadians are taking herbal remedies because they think that natural herbs are safe, but herbal remedies can cause bad reactions when they blunt prescriptions or interact with other health products.

Put key ideas at the beginning and end of sentences

Read these sentences aloud:

1   This experiment tests a variety of antimicrobial agents on a range of microorganisms to collect information about antibiotic resistance.

2   This experiment collects information on antibiotic resistance by testing a variety of antimicrobial agents on a range of microorganisms.

3   Antibiotic resistance is a growing problem so experiments are important that shed insight into the effects of microbial agents on a range of microorganisms.

Most readers put the most emphasis on the words at the beginning and end of a sentence. This means that information in the middle of a sentence can sometimes get lost. Sentence 1 emphasizes the link between the experiment and antibiotic resistance. Sentence 2 highlights the method used to gain information on this resistance. Sentence 3 emphasizes what antibiotic resistance is—the (negative) effect of microbial agents on microorganisms. Which one you choose depends on your purpose. While readers notice the information at the beginning of a sentence, they remember the words at the end of a sentence, so put new and important information at the end.

21b Forge Links Across Sentences

When your writing maintains a focus of attention across sentences, the reader can distinguish the important ideas and how they relate to each other. To achieve this coherence, you need to control which ideas occupy the positions of greatest emphasis. The words you repeat from sentence to sentence act as links.

Link sentences from front to front

In front-to-front linkage, the subject of the sentence remains the focus in subsequent sentences. In the following sequence, sentence 1 identifies three subjects (tetracycline, erythromycin, and cycloheximide) that are developed further in the paragraph using front-to-front linkage. Tetracycline in sentence 1 is repeated as the subject of sentence 2 and "it" further develops information about tetracycline. Sentence 3 picks up erythromycin as the subject, and sentence 4 uses "it" to link the added information back to the previous sentence. Sentence 5 picks up cycloheximide from sentence 1 and becomes the main subject of the sentence, using "it" to link the additional information about this third drug. Sentence 6 then pulls together the three earlier subjects (tetracycline, erythromycin, and cycloheximide) by providing details that apply to all three drugs.

1   Tetracycline, erythromycin, and cycloheximide all act by inhibiting protein synthesis within the bacterial cell.

2   Tetracycline acts by binding to the 30S subunit of the bacterial ribosome, distorting it so that the tRNA does not line up with the codon on the mRNA.

3   Erythromycin acts on the 50S subunit of the bacterial ribosome, inhibiting translation and consequently protein synthesis.

4   It inhibits growth for most organisms but actually kills some gram-positive species.

5   Cycloheximide also inhibits protein synthesis, but it acts on the 60S subunit of the eukaryotic ribosome, and because of this, it is very toxic to people.

6   These antibiotics that act by inhibiting protein synthesis have a much broader range of organisms that they can affect than the cell-wall–attacking antibiotics.

Each sentence adds more information about the repeated topics, tetracycline, erythromycin, and cycloheximide.

Link sentences from back to front

In back-to-front linkage, use new information at the end of one sentence as the subject of the next sentence. This type of linkage allows you to introduce new material and comment on it.

1   One antibiotic that works by inhibiting protein synthesis within the bacterial cell is erythromycin.

2   Erythromycin acts on the 50S subunit of the bacterial ribosome, inhibiting translation and consequently protein synthesis.

3   While it inhibits protein synthesis and therefore growth for most organisms, it actually kills some gram-positive species.

Back-to-front linkage is useful when you need to advance ideas quickly—for example, when you are telling stories. It is also useful for leading readers through a complex sequence of ideas. Rarely, however, will you use either front-to-front linkage or back-to-front linkage continuously throughout a piece of writing. Use front-to-front linkage to add more information and back-to-front linkage to move the topic along.

Check the links between your sentences to find any gaps that will cause your readers to stumble.

21c   Use Parallel Structure with Parallel Ideas

What if Nellie McClung had said, "Don't bother taking back your point, apologizing, or explaining, but get the work finished and ignore their howling"? Would we remember those words today? Many of us do remember the words she did write: "Never retract, never apologize, never explain—get the thing done and let them howl." Writers who use parallel structure often create memorable sentences. Using parallel structure can also help your readers understand your ideas more easily.

Use parallelism with coordinating conjunctions and correlative conjunctions

When you join elements with coordinating conjunctions (*and, or, yet, so, but, for*) use parallel grammatical structure for these elements. Similarly, when you use correlative conjunctions (*either ... or; neither ... nor; not only ... but also; whether ... or*) use identical structure in these constructions.

Awkward

In the global economy, the method of production and where factories are located has become unimportant compared to the creation of new concepts and marketing those concepts.

Parallel

In the global economy, how we make *and* produce goods has become unimportant compared to how we create *and* market new concepts.

Use parallelism for items in a list

Make items in a list parallel in structure to help readers understand and remember them.

Awkward

The 2011 earthquake and tsunami in Japan identified three problems with the country's nuclear generating plants: they were earthquake-proof but not earthquake-plus-tsunami-proof; backup generators malfunctioned when swamped by saltwater; and fuel rods were overheated by total power failure, which caused the structures to rupture, and emitted radiation.

Parallel

The 2011 earthquake and tsunami in Japan identified three problems with the country's nuclear generating plants: the plants withstood the earthquake but not the tsunami that followed; the backup generators malfunctioned when swamped by saltwater; and fuel rods overheated when all power failed, the structures ruptured, and radiation leaked.

The more structural elements you match, the stronger the effect the parallelism will achieve.

COMMON ERRORS

Faulty parallel structure

When writers neglect to use parallel structure, the result can be jarring. To help you catch problems in parallelism, read your writing aloud. Try reading this sentence aloud:

> At our club meeting we identified problems in finding new members, publicizing our activities, and maintenance of our website.

The end of the sentence does not sound right because the parallel structure is broken. We expect to find another verb + *ing* following *finding* and *publicizing*. Instead, we run into *maintenance*, a noun. The problem is easy to fix: change the noun to the *-ing* verb form.

> At our club meeting we identified problems in finding new members, publicizing our activities, and maintaining our website.

Remember: Use parallel structure for parallel elements within a sentence.

22 | Finding the Right Words

QUICKTAKE

- Choose the right level of formality (see pp. 193–194)
- Write to be inclusive (see p. 195)

Suppose you want to e-mail a friend about a new song you heard on the radio. You might be impressed by the words, which you praise to your friend. Now imagine in your English class you are asked to find an example of common poetry, such as song lyrics or an advertising jingle, and to describe that poetry. You realize the song you like will fulfill the assignment, and you write about the lyrics. The language you use in each case will likely be very different.

In the e-mail to your friend, you might use contractions and slang to describe the music. In the school assignment, and in most workplace writing, you will probably use what writers call standard written Canadian English.

22a Recognize Varieties of English

As a general concept, **standard written Canadian English** is a dialect that is used in most academic, business, and public contexts. We use this dialect when we wish to be understood by the widest possible audience. That goal requires that we eliminate, or at least explain, words that have particular meanings for particular groups, and especially words that are used only by certain groups. You will write most of your post-secondary assignments in standard written Canadian English, the variety of English that is best suited for a broad post-secondary audience in Canada.

Jargon

Jargon is the specialized language of a discipline or occupation. Using jargon in appropriate situations can be an effective way to communicate. When you start a new job or a new class, you often must learn a new jargon—words specific to that particular activity or field of study.

Your decision about when to use discipline-specific language in place of words a general audience would understand will depend on your audience. A doctor can say to another doctor, "The X-rays show a fracture in the fifth metatarsal." But a patient might prefer that the doctor say, "Your foot is fractured." Jargon is often the most efficient and precise way for experts in a field to communicate. However, to a nonexpert audience, jargon may sound self-important if common language would do just as well. Avoid using jargon when writing to nonexpert readers. An exception is when your audience needs to learn important key terms. In such cases, be sure to define the specialized terms that your readers may not know.

Euphemisms

Euphemisms are rephrasings of harsh terms; they attempt to avoid offending or to skirt an unpleasant issue. For instance, the provincial government in Ontario makes all employees pay what they call a "health care premium" when the extra charge is, in fact, a tax. A well-chosen euphemism can be tactful in a sensitive situation. A bereaved person might rather hear, "I was sorry to hear of your grandmother's passing" than "I was sorry to hear your grandmother died." However, poorly chosen euphemisms can hurt a writer's ethos if they are used to make excuses or downplay the sufferings of others.

22b Be Aware of Levels of Formality

While you may get plenty of practice in informal writing—e-mails and notes to friends and family members—mastering formal writing is essential in academic and professional settings. How formal or informal should your writing be? That depends on your audience and the writing task at hand.

Decide how formal your writing should be
- Who is your audience?
- What is the occasion?
- What level of formality is your audience accustomed to in similar situations?
- What impression of yourself do you want to give?

Colloquialisms

Colloquialisms are words or expressions that are used informally, often in conversation but less often in writing.

> I'm not happy with my marks, but that's the way the cookie crumbles.

> Caroline worships the ground Sharon walks on.

> I enjoyed the restaurant, but it was nothing to write home about.

> I think Sue got up on the wrong side of the bed today.

In academic and professional writing, colloquialisms can suggest a flippant attitude, a lack of sophistication, or even thoughtlessness. Sometimes colloquialisms can be used for ironic or humorous effect, but as a general rule, if you want to be taken seriously, avoid using them.

At the same time, formality does not mean being pretentious or wordy.

Wordy

The details of the visuals that are overlooked in general such as the scales on graphs received extra attention from me.

Better

I carefully analyzed the generally overlooked details of the visuals, such as the graph scales.

Slang

The most conspicuous kind of language to avoid in formal writing is *slang*. Slang words are created by and for a particular group—even if that group is just you and your friend.

Sorry I'm late; a minivan car-b-q on the 401 blocked all three lanes.

Friday night we were grillin' n chillin' with the crew.

Slang is used to indicate membership in a particular group, and usually to exclude other groups. For that reason avoid using slang in academic writing.

22c Be Aware of Denotation and Connotation

Words have both literal meanings, called **denotations**, and associated meanings, called **connotations**. The contrast is evident in words that mean roughly the same thing but have different connotations. For example, some people are set in their opinions, a quality that can be described positively as *persistent, firm*, and *steadfast* or negatively as *stubborn, bullheaded*, and *close-minded*.

In post-secondary and professional writing, writers should not rely on the connotations of words to support arguments. For example, the statement *It's only common sense to fund education adequately* substitutes positive connotations for evidence. What is *common sense* for one person, however, is not common sense for another, and how *adequately* is defined varies greatly. This statement is not an effective argument in post-secondary writing because it relies on connotation in place of persuasive evidence and effective support.

22d Use Specific Language

Be precise

Effective writing conveys information clearly and precisely. Words such as *situation, sort, thing, aspect,* and *kind* often signal undeveloped or even lazy thinking.

Vague	The violence aspect determines how video games are rated.
Better	The level of violence determines how video games are rated.

When citing numbers or quantities, be as exact as possible. A precise number, if known, is always better than slippery words like *several* or *many,* which some writers use to cloak the fact that they don't know the exact quantity.

Use a dictionary

There is no greater tool for writers than the dictionary. Always have a dictionary handy when you write—either a book or an online version—and get into the habit of using it. In addition to checking spelling, you can find additional meanings of a word that perhaps you had not considered, and you can find the etymology—the origins of a word. In many cases knowing the etymology of a word can help you use it to better effect. For example, if you want to argue that universities as institutions have succeeded because they bring people together in contexts that prepare them for their lives after graduation, you might point out the etymology of *university. University* can be traced back to the late Latin word *universitas,* which means "society or guild," thus emphasizing the idea of a community of learning.

22e Write to Be Inclusive

While the conventions of inclusiveness change continually, three guidelines for inclusive language toward all groups remain constant:

- Do not point out people's differences unless those differences are relevant to your argument.

- Call people whatever *they* prefer to be called.
- When given a choice of terms, choose the more accurate one. (*Vietnamese*, for example, is preferable to *Asian*.)

Be inclusive about gender

Don't use masculine nouns and pronouns to refer to both men and women. *He, his, him, man*, and *mankind* are outmoded and inaccurate terms for both genders. Eliminate gender bias by following these tips:

- Don't say *boy* when you could say *child*.
- Use *men and women* or *people* for generic people, instead of *men*.
- Use *humanity* or *humankind* in place of *mankind*.

Eliminating *he, his*, and *him* when referring to both men and women is more complicated. Many readers consider *he/she* to be an awkward alternative. Try one of the following instead:

- Make the noun and its corresponding pronoun plural. The pronoun will change from *he, him*, or *his* to *they, them*, or *theirs*.

Biased Masculine Pronouns

An undercover agent won't reveal his identity, even to other agents, if he thinks it will jeopardize the case.

Better

Undercover agents won't reveal their identities, even to other agents, if they think it will jeopardize the case.

- Replace the pronoun with an article (*the, a*, or *an*)

Biased Masculine Pronoun

Each prospective driving instructor must pass a provincial test before receiving his licence.

Better

Each prospective driving instructor must pass a provincial test before receiving a licence.

Professional titles that indicate gender—*chairman, waitress*—falsely imply that the gender of the person doing the job changes the essence of the job being done. Use gender-neutral terms for professions. *Chair* and *server* are common gender-neutral alternatives to *chairman* and *waitress*. Terms like *woman doctor* and *male nurse* imply that a woman working as a doctor and a man working as a nurse are abnormal. Instead, write simply *doctor* and *nurse*.

Be inclusive about race and ethnicity

Use the terms for racial and ethnic groups that the groups use for themselves. For example, use *native peoples* or *Aboriginals* to refer to members of Canada's First Nations and *Inuit* to write about native peoples of the Far North.

If you are still in doubt, err on the side of specificity. Broad regional terms (*European, African, Caribbean*) are inaccurate because they do not acknowledge the uniqueness of each nation within the region. *Asian* is currently preferred over *Oriental*; however, more specific terms like *Vietnamese* and *Japanese* are preferred.

Be inclusive about people with disabilities

The *Publication Manual of the American Psychological Association* (5th ed.) offers some good advice: "Put people first, not their disability" (75). Write *people who are deaf* instead of *the deaf* and *a student who is quadriplegic* instead of *a quadriplegic student*.

Be inclusive about people of different ages

Avoid bias by choosing accurate terms to describe age. If possible, use the person's age. *Eighty-two-year-old Adele Schumacher* is better than *elderly Adele Schumacher*.

5 Grammar

23 Fragments, Run-ons, and Comma Splices

QUICKTAKE

- Identify and correct fragments (see below)
- Identify and correct run-on sentences (see p. 202)
- Identify and correct comma splices (see p. 204)

23a Fragments

Fragments are incomplete sentences. They are punctuated to look like sentences, but they lack a key element—often a subject or a verb—or else they are a subordinate clause or phrase. Consider an example of a full sentence followed by a fragment:

> The university's enrolment rose unexpectedly during the fall semester. **Because the percentage of students who accepted offers of admission was much higher than previous years and fewer students than usual dropped out or transferred.**

When a sentence starts with *because*, we expect to find a main clause later. Instead, the *because* clause here refers back to the previous sentence. The writer no doubt knew that the fragment gave reasons why enrolment rose, but a reader must stop to determine the connection.

In formal writing you should avoid fragments. Readers expect words punctuated as a sentence to be a complete sentence. They expect writers to complete their thoughts rather than force readers to guess the missing element.

Basic strategies for turning fragments into sentences

Incorporate the fragment into an adjoining sentence. In many cases you can add the fragment to an adjoining sentence.

I was hooked on the ~~game. Playing~~ day and night.

Add the missing element. If you cannot incorporate a fragment into another sentence, add the missing element.

investors   should think
When aiming for the highest returns, ~~and also thinking~~ about the possible losses.

COMMON ERRORS

Recognizing fragments

If you can spot fragments, you can fix them. Grammar checkers can find some of them, but they miss many fragments and may identify other sentences wrongly as fragments. Ask these questions when you are checking for sentence fragments.

- **Does the sentence have a subject?** Except for commands, sentences need subjects:

  Incorrect   Jane spent every cent of credit she had available. And then applied for more cards.

- **Does the sentence have a complete verb?** Sentences require complete verbs. Verbs that end in *-ing* must have an auxiliary verb to be complete.

  Incorrect   Ralph keeps changing majors. He trying to figure out what he really wants to do after college.

- **If the sentence begins with a subordinate clause, is there a main clause in the same sentence?**

  Incorrect   Even though Seattle is cloudy much of the year, no American city is more beautiful when the sun shines. Which is one reason people continue to move there.

Remember:
1. A sentence must have a subject and a complete verb.
2. A subordinate clause cannot stand alone as a sentence.

23b Run-on Sentences

While fragments are incomplete sentences, run-ons jam together two or more sentences, failing to separate them with appropriate punctuation.

Fixing run-on sentences

Take three steps to fix run-on sentences: (1) identify the problem, (2) determine where the run-on sentence needs to be divided, and (3) choose the punctuation that indicates the relationship between the main clauses.

COMMON ERRORS

Recognizing run-on sentences

When you read this sentence, you realize something is wrong.

Incorrect   I do not recall what kind of printer it was all I remember is that it could sort, staple, and print a packet at the same time.

The problem is that two main clauses are not separated by punctuation. The reader must look carefully to determine where one main clause stops and the next one begins.

> I do not recall what kind of printer it was | all I remember is that it could sort, staple, and print a packet at the same time.

A period should be placed after *was*, and the next sentence should begin with a capital letter:

Correct   I do not recall what kind of printer it was. All I remember is that it could sort, staple, and print a packet at the same time.

Run-on sentences are major errors.

Remember: Two main clauses must be separated by correct punctuation.

1. Identify the problem. When you read your writing aloud, run-on sentences will often trip you up, just as they confuse readers. Search for subject and verb pairs to check for run-ons. If you find two main clauses with no punctuation separating them, you have a run-on sentence.

┌──────SUBJ──────┐ ┌──VERB──┐
Internet businesses are not bound to specific locations or old
                                  ┌ S ┐┌ V ┐
ways of running a business **they** are more flexible in allowing

employees to telecommute and to determine the hours they work.

2. Determine where the run-on sentence needs to be divided.

Internet businesses are not bound to specific locations or old ways of running a business | they are more flexible in allowing employees to telecommute and to determine the hours they work.

3. Determine the relationship between the main clauses. You will revise a run-on more effectively if you first determine the relationship between the main clauses and understand the effect or point you are trying to make. There are several punctuation strategies for fixing run-ons.

- **Insert a period.** This is the simplest way to fix a run-on sentence.

  Internet businesses are not bound to specific locations or old ways of running a business. They are more flexible in allowing employees to telecommute and to determine the hours they work.

  However, if you want to indicate a closer relationship between the two main clauses, you may want to choose one of the following strategies.

- **Insert a semicolon (and possibly a transitional word indicating the relationship between the two main clauses).**

  Internet businesses are not bound to specific locations or old ways of running a business; therefore, they are more flexible in allowing employees to telecommute and to determine the hours they work.

● **Insert a comma and a coordinating conjunction (*and, but, or, nor, for, so, yet*).**

Internet businesses are not bound to specific locations or old ways of running a business, so they are more flexible in allowing employees to telecommute and to determine the hours they work.

● **Make one of the clauses subordinate.**

Because internet businesses are not bound to specific locations or old ways of running a business, they are more flexible in allowing employees to telecommute and to determine the hours they work.

23c Comma Splices

Comma splices occur when two or more sentences are incorrectly joined by a comma: a comma links two clauses that could stand on their own. In this example, the comma following "classes" should be a period.

> Most of us were taking the same classes, if someone had a question, we would all help out.

Such sentences include a punctuation mark—a comma—separating two main clauses. However, a comma is not a strong enough punctuation mark to separate two main clauses.

Fixing comma splices

You have several options for fixing comma splices. Select the one that best fits where the sentence is located and the effect you are trying to achieve.

1. Change the comma to a period. Most comma splices can be fixed by changing the comma to a period.

> It didn't matter that I worked in a windowless room for 40 hours a
> week. On
> ~~week, on~~ the web I was exploring and learning more about distant
> people and places than I ever had before.

COMMON ERRORS

Recognizing comma splices

When you edit your writing, look carefully at sentences that contain commas. Does the sentence contain two main clauses? If so, are the main clauses joined by a comma and coordinating conjunction (*and, but, for, or, not, so, yet*)?

Incorrect	┌─SUBJ─┐ ┌─VERB─┐ The **concept** of "nature" **depends** on the concept of ┌─SUBJ─┐ ┌V┐ human "culture," the **problem is** that "culture" is itself shaped by "nature." [Two main clauses joined by only a comma]
Correct	Even though the concept of "nature" depends on the concept of human "culture," "culture" is itself shaped by "nature." [Subordinate clause plus a main clause]
Correct	The concept of "nature" depends on the concept of human "culture," but "culture" is itself shaped by "nature." [Two main clauses joined by a comma and coordinating conjunction]

The word *however* produces some of the most common comma splice errors. *However* usually functions to begin a main clause, and it should be punctuated with a semicolon rather than a comma.

Incorrect	The Prime Minister's press secretary repeatedly vowed the government was not choosing a side between the two countries embroiled in conflict, **however** the developing foreign policy suggested otherwise.
Correct	The Prime Minister's press secretary repeatedly vowed the government was not choosing a side between the two countries embroiled in conflict; **however,** the developing foreign policy suggested otherwise. [Two main clauses joined by a semicolon]

Remember: Do not use a comma as a period.

2. Change the comma to a semicolon. A semicolon indicates the close connection between the two main clauses.

Next the fluorophores on the slide were exposed to ~~photobleaching,~~ *photobleaching;* the procedure was aimed at reducing the fluorophore density on the surface.

3. Insert a coordinating conjunction. Other comma splices can be repaired by inserting a coordinating conjunction (*and, but, or, nor, so, yet, for*) to indicate the relationship of the two main clauses. The coordinating conjunction must be preceded by a comma.

Digital technologies have intensified a global culture that affects us daily in large and small ways, *yet* their impact remains poorly understood.

4. Make one of the main clauses a subordinate clause. If a comma splice includes one main clause that is subordinate to the other, rewrite the sentence using a subordinating conjunction.

Because community ~~Community~~ is the vision of a great society trimmed down to the size of a small town, it is a powerful metaphor for real estate developers who sell a mini-utopia along with a house or condo.

5. Make one of the main clauses a phrase. You can also rewrite one of the main clauses as a phrase.

Community—the vision of a great society trimmed down to the size of a small town—is a powerful metaphor for real estate developers who sell a mini-utopia along with a house or condo.

24 | Subject-Verb Agreement

QUICKTAKE

• Decide whether a subject is singular or plural (see below)
• Choose the right verb for indefinite pronouns (see p. 209)

24a Agreement in the Present Tense

When your verb is in the present tense, agreement in number is straightforward: the subject takes the base form of the verb in all but the third person singular. For example, the verb *walk*, in the present tense, agrees in number with most subjects in its base form:

First person singular	I walk
Second person singular	You walk
First person plural	We walk
Second person plural	You walk
Third person plural	They walk

Third person singular subjects are the exception to this rule. When your subject is in the third person singular (*he, it, Fido, Lucy, Mr. Jones*) you need to add an *s* or *es* to the base form of the verb.

Third person singular (add *s*)	He walks. It walks. Buster walks.
Third person singular (add *es*)	Lucy goes. Mr. Jones goes.

24b Singular and Plural Subjects

Follow these rules when you have trouble determining whether to use a singular or plural verb form.

Subjects joined by *and*

When two subjects are joined by *and*, treat them as a compound (plural) subject.

Both gentamicin and tobramycin are effective against gram-negative organisms.

Some compound subjects are treated as singular. These kinds of compounds generally work together as a single noun. Although they appear to be compound and therefore plural, these subjects take the singular form of the verb:

Rock and roll remains the devil's music, even in the twenty-first century.

When two nouns linked by *and* are modified by *every* or *each*, these two nouns are likewise treated as one singular subject:

Each Tuesday and Thursday is pizza night at Lister Hall.

Subjects joined by *or, either . . . or,* or *neither . . . nor*

If a subject is joined by *or, either . . . or,* or *neither . . . nor*, make sure the verb agrees with the subject closest to the verb.

┌─SING─┐ ┌──PLURAL──┐ ┌PL┐
Is it **the sky or the mountains** that are blue?

┌──PLURAL──┐ ┌─SING─┐ ┌─SING─┐
Is it **the mountains or the sky** that surrounds us?

┌──PLURAL──┐ ┌──SING──┐┌SING┐
Neither the animals nor the zookeeper knows how to relock the

gate.

┌─SING─┐ ┌──PLURAL──┐┌PL┐
Either a coyote or several dogs were howling last night.

Subjects along with another noun

Verbs agree with the subject of a sentence, even when a subject is linked to another noun with a phrase like *as well as, along with,* or *alongside*. These modifying phrases are usually set off from the main subject with commas.

┌────── IGNORE THIS PHRASE ──────┐
Chicken, alongside various steamed vegetables, is my favourite meal.

┌IGNORE THIS PHRASE┐
Besides B. B. King, **John Lee Hooker and Muddy Waters** are my favourite blues artists of all time.

COMMON ERRORS

Subjects separated from verbs

The most common agreement errors occur when words come between the subject and verb. These intervening words do not affect subject-verb agreement. To ensure that you use the correct verb form, identify the subject and the verb. Ignore any phrases that come between them.

┌──IGNORE THIS PHRASE──

Incorrect A recent study showed that **students** at Strathcona High School reads more than suburban students.

Correct A recent study showed that **students** at Strathcona High School read more than suburban students.

Students is plural and *read* is plural; subject and verb agree.

┌──IGNORE THIS PHRASE──┐

Incorrect **The whale shark**, the largest of all sharks, feed on plankton.

Correct **The whale shark**, the largest of all sharks, feeds on plankton.

The plural noun *sharks* that appears between the subject *the whale shark* and the verb *feeds* does not change the number of the subject. The subject is singular and the verb is singular. Subject and verb agree.

Remember: When you check for subject-verb agreement, identify the subject and the verb. Ignore any words that come between them.

24c Indefinite Pronouns as Subjects

The choice of a singular or plural pronoun is determined by the **antecedent**—the noun that the pronoun refers to. Indefinite pronouns, such as *some, few, all, someone, everyone*, and *each*, often do not refer to identifiable subjects; hence they have no antecedents. Most indefinite pronouns are singular and agree with the singular forms of verbs. Some, like *both* and *many*, are always plural and agree with the plural forms of verbs. Other indefinite pronouns are variable and can agree with either singular or plural verb forms, depending on the context of the sentence.

COMMON ERRORS

Agreement errors using *each*

The indefinite pronoun *each* is a frequent source of subject-verb agreement errors. If a pronoun is singular, its verb must be singular. This rule holds true even when the subject is modified by a phrase that includes a plural noun.

A common stumbling block to this rule is the pronoun *each*. *Each* is always treated as a singular pronoun in post-secondary writing. When *each* stands alone, the choice is easy to make:

Incorrect   **Each** are an outstanding student.
Correct   **Each** is an outstanding student.

But when *each* is modified by a phrase that includes a plural noun, the choice of a singular verb form becomes less obvious:

Incorrect   **Each** of the girls are fit.
Correct   **Each** of the girls is fit.

Incorrect   **Each** of our dogs get a present.
Correct   **Each** of our dogs gets a present.

Remember: *Each* is always singular.

24d Collective Nouns as Subjects

Collective nouns refer to groups (*audience, class, committee, crowd, family, government, group, jury, public, team*). When members of a group are considered as a unit, use singular verbs and singular pronouns.

The **crowd** is unusually quiet at the moment, but **it** will get noisy soon.

When members of a group are considered as individuals, use plural verbs and plural pronouns.

The **faculty** have **their** differing opinions on how to address the problems caused by reduced government support.

24e Amounts, Numbers, and Pairs

Subjects that describe amounts of money, time, distance, or measurement are singular and require singular verbs.

Three days is never long enough to unwind.

Some subjects, such as courses of study, academic specializations, illnesses, and even some nations, are treated as singular subjects even though their names end in *s* or *es*. For example, *economics, news, ethics, measles,* and *the United States* all end in *s* but are all singular subjects.

Economics is a rich field of study.

Other subjects require a plural verb form even though they refer to single items such as *jeans, slacks, glasses, scissors,* and *tweezers*. These items are all pairs.

My **glasses** are scratched.

25 | Verbs

QUICKTACE

- Understand basic verb forms (see below)
- Distinguish forms of transitive and intransitive verbs (see p. 215)

25a Basic Verb Forms

Almost all verbs in English have five possible forms. The exception is the verb *be*. Regular verbs follow this basic pattern:

Base form	Third person singular	Past tense	Past participle	Present participle
jump	jumps	jumped	jumped	jumping
like	likes	liked	liked	liking
talk	talks	talked	talked	talking
wish	wishes	wished	wished	wishing

Base form

The base form of the verb is the one you find listed in the dictionary. This form indicates an action or condition in the present.

I **like** Halifax in June.

Third person singular

Third person singular subjects include *he, she, it,* and the nouns they replace, as well as other pronouns, including *someone, anybody,* and *everything.* Present tense verbs in the third person singular end with an *s* or an *es.*

Ms. Nessan **speaks** in riddles.

Past tense

The past tense describes an action or condition that occurred in the past. For most verbs, the past tense is formed by adding *d* or *ed* to the base form of the verb.

She **inhaled** the night air.

Many verbs, however, have irregular past tense forms. (See Section 25b.)

Past participle

The past participle is used with *have* to form verbs in the perfect tense, with *be* to form verbs in the passive voice (see Section 19a), and to form adjectives derived from verbs.

Past perfect	They **had** gone to the grocery store prematurely.
Passive	The book **was** written thirty years before it **was** published.
Adjective	In the eighties, teased hair was all the rage.

COMMON ERRORS

Missing verb endings

Verb endings are not always pronounced in speech, especially in some dialects of English. It's also easy to omit these endings when you are writing quickly. Because spell-checkers will not mark these errors, you have to find them while proofreading.

Incorrect	Jeremy feel as if he's catching a cold.
Correct	Jeremy feels as if he's catching a cold.
Incorrect	Sheila hope she would get the day off.
Correct	Sheila hoped she would get the day off.

Remember: Check verbs carefully for missing *s* or *es* endings in the present tense and missing *d* or *ed* endings in the past tense.

Present participle

The present participle functions in one of three ways. Used with an auxiliary verb, it can describe a continuing action. The present participle can also function as a noun, known as a **gerund**, or as an adjective. The present participle is formed by adding *ing* to the base form of a verb.

Present participle	Wild elks **are** competing for limited food resources.
Gerund	Sailing around the Cape of Good Hope is rumoured to bring good luck.
Adjective	We looked for shells in the ebbing tide.

A verb is **regular** when its past and past participle forms are created by adding *ed* or *d* to the base form. If this rule does not apply, the verb is considered an **irregular** verb. Here are selected common irregular verbs and their basic conjugations.

Common irregular verbs

Base form	Past tense	Past participle
be (is, am, are)	was, were	been
become	became	become
bring	brought	brought
come	came	come
do	did	done
get	got	got or gotten
go	went	gone
have	had	had
know	knew	known
see	saw	seen

COMMON ERRORS

Confusing the past tense and past participle forms of irregular verbs

The past tense and past participle forms of irregular verbs are often confused. The most frequent error is using a past tense form instead of the past participle with *had*.

                         PAST TENSE

Incorrect   She had never **rode** a horse before.

                         PAST PARTICIPLE

Correct   She had never **ridden** a horse before.

                  PAST TENSE

Incorrect   He had **saw** many whales in Nanaimo.

                  PAST PARTICIPLE

Correct   He had **seen** many whales in Nanaimo.

Remember: Change any past tense verbs preceded by *had* to past participles.

Transitive and Intransitive Verbs

Lay/lie and *raise/rise*

Do your house keys lay or lie on the kitchen table? *Raise/rise* and *lay/lie* are transitive and intransitive verbs that writers frequently confuse. Transitive verbs take direct objects—nouns that receive the action of the verb. Intransitive verbs act in sentences that lack direct objects. Chickens lay eggs but people lie down.

The following charts list the trickiest pairs of transitive and intransitive verbs and the correct forms for each verb tense. Pay special attention to *lay* and *lie*, which are irregular.

	lay (put something down)	**lie (recline)**
Present	lay, lays	lie, lies
Present participle	laying	lying
Past	laid	lay
Past participle	laid	lain

Transitive	Once you complete your test, please lay your pencil [direct object, the thing being laid down] on the desk.
Intransitive	The *Titanic* lies upright in two pieces at a depth of 13,000 feet.

	raise (elevate something)	**rise (get up)**
Present	raise, raises	rise, rises
Present participle	raising	rising
Past	raised	rose
Past participle	raised	risen

Transitive	We raise our glasses [direct object, the things being raised] to toast Uncle Han.
Intransitive	The sun rises over the bay.

26 | Pronouns

- Choose the correct pronoun case (see below)
- Identify and correct errors in pronoun agreement (see p. 219)

26a Pronoun Case

Subject pronouns function as the subjects of sentences. **Object pronouns** function as direct or indirect objects. **Possessive pronouns** indicate ownership.

Subject pronouns	Object pronouns	Possessive pronouns
I	me	my, mine
we	us	our, ours
you	you	your, yours
he	him	his
she	her	her, hers
it	it	its
they	them	their, theirs
who	whom	whose

Pronouns in compound phrases

Picking the right pronoun sometimes can be confusing when the pronoun appears in a compound phrase.

> If we work together, you and **me** can get the job done quickly.

> If we work together, you and **I** can get the job done quickly.

Which is correct—*me* or *I*? Removing the other pronoun usually makes the choice clear.

| Incorrect | Me can get the job done quickly. |
| Correct | I can get the job done quickly. |

216

We and *us* before nouns

Another pair of pronouns that can cause difficulty is *we* and *us* before nouns.

Us friends must stick together.

We friends must stick together.

Which is correct—*us* or *we?* Removing the noun indicates the correct choice.

Incorrect   **Us** must stick together.

Correct   **We** must stick together.

Who versus *whom*

Choosing between *who* and *whom* is often difficult, even for experienced writers. The distinction between *who* and *whom* is disappearing from spoken language. *Who* is more often used in spoken language, even when *whom* is correct.

COMMON ERRORS

Who or *Whom*

In writing, the distinction between *who* and *whom* is still often observed. *Who* and *whom* follow the same rules as other pronouns: *Who* is the subject pronoun; *whom* is the object pronoun. If you are dealing with an object, *whom* is the correct choice.

Incorrect   **Who** did you send the letter to?
                Who did you give the present to?

Correct   To **whom** did you send the letter?
           Whom did you give the present to?

Who is always the right choice for the subject pronoun.

Correct   **Who** gave you the present?
          Who brought the cookies?

(Continued on next page)

COMMON ERRORS *(Continued)*

If you are uncertain of which one to use, try substituting *she* and *her* or *he* and *him*.

Incorrect	You sent the letter to **she** [who]?
Correct	You sent the letter to **her** [whom]?
Incorrect	**Him** [Whom] gave you the present?
Correct	**He** [Who] gave you the present?

Remember:
Who = subject
Whom = object

Whoever versus *whomever*

With the rule regarding *who* and *whom* in mind, you can distinguish between *whoever* and *whomever*. Which is correct?

Her warmth touched **whoever** she met.

Her warmth touched **whomever** she met.

In this sentence the pronoun functions as a direct object: Her warmth touched everyone she met, not someone touched her. Thus *whomever* is the correct choice.

Pronouns in comparisons

When you write a sentence using a comparison that includes *than* or *as* followed by a pronoun, usually you will have to think about which pronoun is correct. Which of the following is correct?

Vimala is a faster swimmer than **him**.

Vimala is a faster swimmer than **he**.

The test that will give you the correct answer is to add the verb that finishes the sentence—in this case, *is*.

Incorrect	Vimala is a faster swimmer than him is.
Correct	Vimala is a faster swimmer than he is.

Adding the verb makes the correct choice evident.

Possessive pronouns

Possessive pronouns at times are confusing because possessive nouns are formed with apostrophes but possessive pronouns do not require apostrophes. Pronouns that use apostrophes are always **contractions**.

It's = It is
Who's = Who is
They're = They are

The test for whether to use an apostrophe is to determine whether the pronoun is possessive or a contraction. The most confusing pair is *its* and *it's*.

Incorrect	Its a sure thing she will be elected. [Contraction is wanted.]
Correct	It's a sure thing she will be elected. [**It is** a sure thing.]
Incorrect	The dog lost it's collar. [Possessive is wanted.]
Correct	The dog lost its collar.

26b Pronoun Agreement

Because pronouns usually replace or refer to other nouns, they must match those nouns in number and gender. The noun that the pronoun replaces is called its **antecedent**. If pronoun and antecedent match, they are in **agreement**. When a pronoun is close to the antecedent, usually there is no problem.

Maria forgot her coat.

The band **members** collected their uniforms.

Pronoun agreement errors often happen when pronouns and the nouns they replace are separated by several words.

Incorrect
The **players**, exhausted from the double-overtime game, picked up his sweats and walked toward the locker rooms.

Correct
The **players**, exhausted from the double-overtime game, picked up their sweats and walked toward the locker rooms.

Careful writers make sure that pronouns match their antecedents.

Collective nouns

Collective nouns (such as *audience, class, committee, crowd, family, herd, jury, team*) can be singular or plural depending on whether the emphasis is on the group or on the particular individuals.

Correct   The **committee** was unanimous in its decision.

Correct   The **committee** put their opinions ahead of the goals of the unit.

COMMON ERRORS

Help

Indefinite pronouns

Indefinite pronouns (such as *anybody, anything, each, either, everybody, everything, neither, none, somebody, something*) refer to unspecified people or things. Most take singular pronouns.

Incorrect   **Everybody** can choose their roommates.

Correct   **Everybody** can choose his or her roommate.

Correct
Alternative   **All students** can choose their roommates.

A few indefinite pronouns (*all, any, either, more, most, neither, none, some*) can take either singular or plural pronouns.

Correct   **Some** of the shipment was damaged when it became overheated.

Correct   **All** thought they should have a good seat at the concert.

A few pronouns are always plural (*few, many, several*).

Correct   **Several** want refunds.

Remember: Words that begin with *any, some,* and *every* are usually singular.

COMMON ERRORS

Pronoun agreement with compound antecedents

Antecedents joined by *and* take plural pronouns.

Correct   **Moncef and Driss** practised their music.

Exception: When compound antecedents are preceded by *each* or *every*, use a singular pronoun.

Correct   **Every male cardinal and warbler** arrives before the fe-
male to define its territory.

When compound antecedents are connected by *or* or *nor*, the pronoun agrees with the antecedent closer to it.

Incorrect   **Either the Ross twins or Angela** should bring their games.

Correct   **Either the Ross twins or Angela** should bring her games.

Better   **Either Angela or the Ross twins** should bring their games.

When you put the plural *twins* last, the correct choice becomes the plural pronoun *their*.

Remember:
1. Use plural pronouns for antecedents joined by *and*.
2. Use singular pronouns for antecedents preceded by *each* or *every*.
3. Use a pronoun that agrees with the nearest antecedent when
   compound antecedents are joined by *or* or *nor*.

26c Sexist Pronouns

English does not have a neutral singular pronoun for a group of mixed genders or a person of unknown gender. Referring to a group of mixed genders using male pronouns is unacceptable to many people. Unless the school in the following example is all male, many readers would object to the use of *his*.

| Sexist | **Each student** must select **his** courses using the online registration system. |

One strategy is to use *her or his* or *his or her* instead of *his*.

| Correct | **Each student** must select **his or her** courses using the online registration system. |

Often you can avoid using *his or her* by changing the noun to the plural form.

| Better | **All students** must select **their** courses using the online registration system. |

In some cases, however, using *his or her* is necessary.

26d Vague Reference

Pronouns can sometimes refer to more than one noun, thus confusing readers.

> The **coach** rushed past the injured **player** to yell at the **referee**. **She** was hit in the face by a stray elbow.

You have to guess which person *she* refers to—the coach, the player, or the referee. Sometimes you cannot even guess the antecedent of a pronoun.

> The new subdivision destroyed the last remaining habitat for wildlife within the city limits. **They** have ruined our city with their unchecked greed.

To whom does *they* refer? The mayor and city council? The developers? The people who live in the subdivision? Or all of the above?

Pronouns should never leave the reader guessing about antecedents. If different nouns can be confused as the antecedent, then the ambiguity should be clarified.

| Vague | Mafalda's pet boa constrictor crawled across Tonya's foot. **She** was mortified. |

| Better | When Mafalda's pet boa constrictor crawled across Tonya's foot, **Mafalda** was mortified. |

COMMON ERRORS

Vague use of *this*

Always use a noun immediately after *this, that, these, those,* and *some.*

Vague   Enrique asked Meg to remove the viruses on his computer. This was a bad idea.

Was it a bad idea for Enrique to ask Meg because she was insulted? Because she didn't know how? Because removing viruses would destroy some of Enrique's files?

Better   Enrique asked Meg to remove the viruses on his computer. This imposition on Meg's time made her resentful.

Remember: Ask yourself "*this* what?" and add the noun that *this* refers to.

27 | Shifts

QUICK*TAKE*

- Identify and correct verb tense shifts (see below)
- Identify and correct shifts in mood (see p. 225), voice (see p. 226), and person and number (see p. 226)

27a Shifts in Tense

Appropriate shifts in verb tense

Changes in verb tense are sometimes necessary to indicate a shift in time.

	PAST TENSE	FUTURE TENSE
Past	Because Oda won the lottery, she will quit her job at
to future		PRESENT TENSE
	the hospital as soon as her supervisor finds a qualified

replacement.

COMMON ERRORS

Unnecessary tense shifts

Notice the tense shift in the following example.

Incorrect   In May of 2000 the "I Love You" virus **crippled** the [PAST TENSE]
computer systems of major companies and **irritated** [PAST TENSE]

millions of private computer users. As the virus
generates millions of emails and **erases** millions of [PRESENT TENSE] [PRESENT TENSE]

computer files, companies such as Ford and Time Warner
are forced to shut down their clogged email systems. [PRESENT TENSE]

The second sentence shifts unnecessarily to the present tense, confusing the reader. Did the "I Love You" virus have its heyday several years ago, or is it still wreaking havoc now? Changing the verbs in the second sentence to the past tense eliminates the confusion.

Correct   In May of 2000 the "I Love You" virus **crippled** the [PAST TENSE]
computer systems of major companies and **irritated** [PAST TENSE]

millions of private computer users. As the virus
generated millions of emails and **erased** millions of [PAST TENSE] [PAST TENSE]

computer files, companies such as Ford and Time Warner
were forced to shut down their clogged email systems. [PAST TENSE]

Remember: Shift verb tense only when you are referring to different time periods.

Inappropriate shifts in verb tense

Be careful to avoid confusing your reader with unnecessary shifts in verb tense.

Incorrect   While Brazil **looks** to ecotourism to fund rain forest [PAST TENSE]
preservation, other South American nations **relied** on [PAST TENSE]

foreign aid and conservation efforts.

The shift from present tense (*looks*) to past tense (*relied*) is confusing. Correct the mistake by putting both verbs in the present tense.

Correct
PRESENT TENSE
While Brazil looks to ecotourism to fund rain forest
PRESENT TENSE
preservation, other South American nations rely on

foreign aid and conservation efforts.

27b Shifts in Mood

Verbs can be categorized into three moods—indicative, imperative, and subjunctive—defined by the functions they serve.

- **Indicative verbs** state facts, opinions, and questions.

  Fact Canadian scientists are mapping the ocean floor
  to strengthen Canada's claim in the Arctic.

- **Imperative verbs** make commands, give advice, and make requests.

  Command Map the ocean floor to strengthen Canada's claim
  in the Arctic.

- **Subjunctive verbs** express wishes, unlikely or untrue situations, hypothetical situations, requests with *that* clauses, and suggestions.

  Unlikely or If just laying claim to the Arctic were enough,
  Untrue Canadian scientists wouldn't need to map the
  Situation ocean floor.

Be careful not to shift from one mood to another in midsentence.

Incorrect If the government were to shift priorities away from
mapping the Arctic Ocean floor, Canadians lose a
chance to assert their sovereignty in the Arctic.

The sudden shift from subjunctive to indicative mood in this sentence is confusing. Are Canadians losing the chance now, or is losing the chance a likely result of the shift in government priorities? Revise the sentence to keep both verbs in the subjunctive.

Correct If the government were to shift priorities away from
mapping the Arctic Ocean floor, Canadians would lose
a chance to assert their sovereignty in the Arctic.

27c Shifts in Voice

Watch for unintended shifts from active (*I ate the cookies*) to passive voice (*the cookies were eaten*).

Incorrect   The sudden storm **toppled** several trees and numerous windows **were shattered.**

The unexpected shift from active voice (*toppled*) to passive (*were broken*) forces readers to wonder whether it was the sudden storm, or something else, that broke the windows.

Correct   The sudden storm **toppled** several trees and **shattered** numerous windows.

Revising the sentence to eliminate the shift to passive voice (see Section 19a) also improves its parallel structure (see 21c).

27d Shifts in Person and Number

Sudden shifts from third person (*he, she, it, one*) to first (*I, we*) or second (*you*) are confusing to readers and often indicate a writer's uncertainty about how to address a reader. We often make such shifts in spoken English, but in formal writing shifts in person need to be recognized and corrected.

Incorrect   When **one** is reading a magazine, **you** often see several different type fonts used on a single page.

The shift from third person to second person in this sentence is confusing.

Correct   When reading a magazine **you** often see several different type fonts used on a single page.

28 | Modifiers

QUICK_TAKE_

- Use the correct form of comparatives and superlatives (see below)
- Identify and correct dangling modifiers (see p. 232)

Modifiers come in two varieties: adjectives and adverbs. The same words can function as adjectives or adverbs, depending on what they modify.

Adjectives modify

nouns—_iced_ tea, _power_ forward
pronouns—He is _brash_.

Adverbs modify

verbs—_barely_ reach, drive _carefully_
adjectives—_truly_ brave activist, _shockingly_ red lipstick
other adverbs—_not_ soon forget, _very_ well
clauses—_Honestly_, I find ballet boring.

Adjectives answer the questions _Which one? How many?_ and _What kind?_ Adverbs answer the questions _How often? To what extent? When? Where? How?_ and _Why?_

28a Choose the Correct Modifier

Use the correct forms of comparatives and superlatives

Comparative modifiers weigh one thing against another. They either end in _er_ or are preceded by _more_.

Road bikes are faster on pavement than mountain bikes.

The more courageous juggler tossed flaming torches.

Superlative modifiers compare three or more items. They either end in _est_ or are preceded by _most_.

April is the hottest month in New Delhi.

Wounded animals are the most ferocious.

When should you add a suffix instead of *more* or *most*? The following guidelines work in most cases:

Adjectives

- For adjectives of one or two syllables, add *er* or *est*.
  redder, heaviest
- For adjectives of three or more syllables, use *more* or *most*.
  more viable, most powerful

Adverbs

- For adverbs of one syllable, use *er* or *est*.
  nearer, slowest
- For adverbs with two or more syllables, use *more* or *most*.
  more convincingly, most humbly

Some frequently used comparatives and superlatives are irregular. The following list can help you become familiar with them.

Adjective	Comparative	Superlative
good	better	best
bad	worse	worst
little (amount)	less	least
many, much	more	most

Adverb	Comparative	Superlative
well	better	best
badly	worse	worst

Do not use both a suffix (*er* or *est*) and *more* or *most*.

Incorrect   The service at Jane's Restaurant is more slower than the service at Alphonso's.

Correct   The service at Jane's Restaurant is slower than the service at Alphonso's.

Absolute modifiers are words that represent an unvarying condition and thus are not subject to the degrees that comparative and superlative constructions convey. Common absolute modifiers include *complete, ultimate,* and *unique. Unique,* for example, means "one of a kind." There's nothing else like it. Thus something cannot be *very unique* or *totally unique.* It is either unique or it is not. Absolute modifiers should not be modified by comparatives (*more* + modifier or modifier + *er*) or superlatives (*most* + modifier or modifier + *est*).

Double negatives

In English, as in mathematics, two negatives equal a positive. Avoid using two negative words in one sentence, or you'll end up saying the opposite of what you mean. The following are negative words that you should avoid doubling up:

barely	nobody	nothing
hardly	none	scarcely
neither	no one	

Incorrect, Double negative	Barely no one noticed that the pop star lip synched during the whole performance.
Correct, Single negative	Barely anyone noticed that the pop star lip synched during the whole performance.
Incorrect, Double negative	When the pastor asked if anyone had objections to the marriage, nobody said nothing.
Correct, Single negative	When the pastor asked if anyone had objections to the marriage, nobody said anything.

28b Place Adjectives Carefully

As a general rule, the closer you place a modifier to the word it modifies, the less likely the chance you will confuse your reader.

Confusing	Watching from the ground below, the kettle of broadwing hawks circled high above the observers.

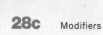
Is the kettle of hawks watching from the ground below? You can fix the problem by putting the modified subject immediately after the modifier or placing the modifier next to the modified subject.

Better   The kettle of broadwing hawks circled high above the **observers** who were watching from the ground below.

Better   Watching from the ground below, the **observers** saw a kettle of broadwing hawks circle high above them.

28c Place Adverbs Carefully

Single-word adverbs and adverbial clauses and phrases can usually sit comfortably either before or after the words they modify.

Dimitri quietly **walked** down the hall.

Dimitri **walked** quietly down the hall.

Conjunctive adverbs—*also, however, instead, likewise, then, therefore, thus*, and others—are adverbs that show how ideas relate to one another. They prepare a reader for contrasts, exceptions, additions, conclusions, and other shifts in an argument. Conjunctive adverbs can usually fit well into more than one place in the sentence. In the following example, *however* could fit in three different places.

Between two main clauses

Professional hockey players earn exorbitant salaries; however, they pay for their wealth with lifetimes of chronic pain and debilitating injuries.

Within second main clause

Professional hockey players earn exorbitant salaries; they pay for their wealth, however, with lifetimes of chronic pain and debilitating injuries.

At end of second main clause

Professional hockey players earn exorbitant salaries; they pay for their wealth with lifetimes of chronic pain and debilitating injuries, however.

COMMON ERRORS

Placement of limiting modifiers

Words such as *almost, even, hardly, just, merely, nearly, not, only,* and *simply* are called **limiting modifiers**. Although people often play fast and loose with their placement in everyday speech, limiting modifiers should always go immediately before the word or words they modify. Many writers have difficulty with the placement of *only*. Like other limiting modifiers, *only* should be placed immediately before the word it modifies.

Incorrect	The Gross Domestic Product only gives one indicator of economic growth.
Correct	The Gross Domestic Product gives only one indicator of economic growth.

The word *only* modifies *one* in this sentence, not *gives*.

Remember: Place limiting modifiers immediately before the word(s) they modify.

28d Use Hyphens with Compound Modifiers

When to hyphenate

- **Hyphenate a compound modifier that precedes a noun.**

  When a compound modifier precedes a noun, you should usually hyphenate the modifier. A **compound modifier** consists of words that join together as a unit to modify a noun.

  middle-class values   self-fulfilling prophecy

- **Hyphenate a phrase when it is used as a modifier that precedes a noun.**

  out-of-body experience   step-by-step instructions

- **Hyphenate the prefixes** *pro-, anti-, post-, pre-, neo-,* **and** *mid-* **before proper nouns.**

  neo-Nazi racism   anti-NAFTA protests

- **Hyphenate a compound modifier with a number when it precedes a noun.**

  eighteenth-century drama   one-way street

When not to hyphenate

- **Do not hyphenate a compound modifier that follows a noun.**

  The instructor's approach is student centred.

- **Do not hyphenate compound modifiers when the first word is** *very* **or ends in** *ly.*

  newly recorded data   very cold day

 Revise Dangling Modifiers

Some modifiers are ambiguous because they could apply to more than one word or clause. **Dangling modifiers** are ambiguous for the opposite reason; they don't have a word to modify. In such cases the modifier is usually an introductory clause or phrase. What is being modified should immediately follow the phrase, but in the following sentence it is absent.

After bowling a perfect game, Surfside Lanes hung Marco's photo on the wall.

You can eliminate a dangling modifier in two ways:

1. Insert the noun or pronoun being modified immediately after the introductory modifying phrase.

   After bowling a perfect game, Marco was honoured by having his photo hung on the wall at Surfside Lanes.

2. Rewrite the introductory phrase as an introductory clause to include the noun or pronoun.

After Marco bowled a perfect game, Surfside Lanes hung his photo on the wall.

COMMON ERRORS

Dangling modifiers

A dangling modifier does not seem to modify anything in a sentence; it dangles, unconnected to the word or words it presumably is intended to modify. Frequently, it produces funny results:

When still a girl, my father joined the army.

It sounds like *my father* was once a girl. The problem is that the subject, *I*, is missing:

When I was still a girl, my father joined the army.

Remember: Modifiers should be clearly connected to the words they modify, especially at the beginning of sentences.

---

29 | Grammar for Multilingual Speakers

QUICKTAKE

- Understand the types of English nouns (see p. 234)
- Use articles correctly (see p. 235)
- Use verbs correctly (see p. 236)

29a Nouns

Perhaps the most troublesome conventions for nonnative speakers are those that guide usage of the common articles *the, a,* and *an.* To understand how articles work in English, you must first understand how the language uses **nouns.**

Kinds of nouns

There are two basic kinds of nouns. A **proper noun** begins with a capital letter and names a unique person, place, or thing: *Rick Mercer, Russia, Eiffel Tower.*

The other basic kind of noun is called a **common noun.** Common nouns do not name a unique person, place, or thing: *man, country, tower.*

Count and noncount nouns

Common nouns can be classified as either *count* or *noncount.* **Count nouns** can be made plural, usually by adding *s* (*finger, fingers*) or by using their plural forms (*person, people; datum, data*). **Noncount nouns** cannot be counted directly and cannot take the plural form (*information,* but not *informations; garbage,* but not *garbages; research*). Some nouns can be either count or noncount, depending on how they are used. *Hair* can refer to either a strand of hair, where it serves as a count noun, or a mass of hair, where it becomes a noncount noun.

COMMON ESL ERRORS

Singular and plural forms of count nouns

Count nouns are simpler to quantify than noncount nouns. But remember that English requires you to state both singular and plural forms of nouns consistently and explicitly. Look at the following sentences.

Incorrect   The three bicyclist shaved their leg before the big race.

Correct   The three bicyclists shaved their legs before the big race.

Remember: English requires you to use plural forms of count nouns even if a plural number is not otherwise indicated.

Articles

Articles indicate that a noun is about to appear, and they clarify what the noun refers to. There are only two kinds of articles in English, definite and indefinite:

1. **the:** *The* is a **definite article**, meaning that it refers to (1) a specific object already known to the reader, (2) one about to be made known to the reader, or (3) a unique object.

2. **a, an:** The **indefinite articles** *a* and *an* refer to an object whose specific identity is not known to the reader. The only difference between *a* and *an* is that *a* is used before a consonant sound (*woman, friend, yellow*), while *an* is used before a vowel sound (*animal, enemy, orange*).

Look at the following two sentences, from a paragraph in a scientific journal article; pay attention to the use of articles.

From a theoretical perspective, a two-dimensional photon counting histogram (PCH) does not offer a conceptually different approach to the analysis from a three-dimensional one.

On the contrary, it uses the same underlying physical phenomena and logic as the original PCH.

The first sentence introduces a discussion of two-dimensional PCH compared to three-dimensional PCH; since it is the first mention of this technique in the paragraph, the indefinite article *a* is appropriate to introduce the discussion in each case. However, in the second sentence, the articles shift to definite ones, *the*, because they refer to the phenomena mentioned in the previous sentence. If the noun has already been mentioned or if it refers to something specific or unique, choose the definite article, *the*. If the noun refers to something general or not previously mentioned, choose the indefinite article, *a* or *an*.

COMMON ESL ERRORS

Articles with count and noncount nouns

Knowing how to distinguish between count and noncount nouns can help you decide which article to use. Noncount nouns are never used with the indefinite articles *a* and *an*.

Incorrect	Maria jumped into a water.
Correct	Maria jumped into the water.

No articles are used with noncount and plural count nouns when you wish to state something that has a general application.

Incorrect	The water is a precious natural resource.
Correct	Water is a precious natural resource.

Remember:
1. Noncount nouns are never used with *a* and *an*.
2. Noncount and plural nouns used to make general statements do not take articles.

29c Verbs

The verb system in English can be divided between simple verbs like *run, speak,* and *look,* and verb phrases like *may have run, have spoken,* and *will be looking.* In these examples, the words that appear before the main verbs—*may, have, will,* and *be*—are called **auxiliary verbs** (also called **helping verbs**).

Indicating tense and voice with *be* verbs

Like the other auxiliary verbs *have* and *do, be* changes form to signal tense. In addition to *be* itself, the **be verbs** are *is, am, are, was, were,* and *been.* To show ongoing action, *be* verbs are followed by the present participle, which is a verb with an *ing* ending:

Incorrect	I am think of all the things I'd rather be do.
Correct	I am thinking of all the things I'd rather be doing.

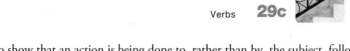

To show that an action is being done to, rather than by, the subject, follow *be* verbs with the past participle (a verb usually ending in *ed, en,* or *t*):

Incorrect   The movie was direct by John Woo.

Correct   The movie was directed by John Woo.

Modal auxiliary verbs

Modal auxiliary verbs *will, would, can, could, may, might, shall, must,* and *should* express conditions like possibility, permission, speculation, expectation, obligation, and necessity. Unlike the auxiliary verbs *be, have,* and *do,* modal verbs do not change form based on the grammatical subject of the sentence (*I, you, she, he, it, we, they*).

Two basic rules apply to all uses of modal verbs. First, modal verbs are always followed by the simple form of the verb. The simple form is the verb by itself, in the present tense, such as *have* but not *had, having,* or *to have.*

Incorrect   She should studies harder to pass the exam.

Correct   She should study harder to pass the exam.

The second rule is that you should not use modals consecutively.

Incorrect   If you work harder at writing, you might could improve.

Correct   If you work harder at writing, you might improve.

Ten conditions that modals express

- **Speculation:** If you flew, you would arrive earlier.
- **Ability:** She can run faster than Jennifer.
- **Necessity:** You must know what you want to do.
- **Intention:** He will wash his own clothes.
- **Permission:** You may leave now.
- **Advice:** You should wash behind your ears.
- **Possibility:** It might be possible to go home early.
- **Assumption:** You must love living in Montreal.
- **Expectation:** You should enjoy the movie.
- **Order:** You must leave the building.

Phrasal verbs

The liveliest and most colourful feature of the English language, its numerous idiomatic phrasal verbs, gives many multilingual speakers the greatest difficulty.

Phrasal verbs consist of a verb and one or two **particles:** either a preposition or an adverb, or both. The verb and particles combine to form a phrase with a particular meaning that is often quite distinct from the meaning of the verb itself. Consider the following sentence.

I need to go over the chapter once more before the test.

Here, the meaning of *go over*—a verb and a preposition that, taken together, suggest casual study—is only weakly related to the meaning of either *go* or *over* by itself. English has hundreds of such idiomatic constructions, and the best way to familiarize yourself with them is to listen to and read as much informal English as you can.

Like regular verbs, phrasal verbs can be either transitive (they take a direct object) or intransitive. In the preceding example, *go over* is transitive. *Quiet down*—as in *Please quiet down*—is intransitive. Some phrases, like *wake up*, can be both: *Wake up!* is intransitive, while *Jenny, wake up the children* is transitive.

In some transitive phrasal verbs, the particles can be separated from the verb without affecting the meaning: *I made up a song* is equivalent to *I made a song up*. In others, the particles cannot be separated from the verb.

Incorrect   You shouldn't play with love around.

Correct   You shouldn't play around with love.

Unfortunately, there are no shortcuts for learning which verbal phrases are separable and which are not. As you become increasingly familiar with English, you will grow more confident in your ability to use phrasal verbs.

PART

6

Punctuation and Mechanics

30 | Commas

- Set off parts of sentences with commas (see below)
- Use commas correctly with quotations (see p. 247)
- Avoid unnecessary commas (see p. 249)

Commas give readers vital clues about how to read a sentence. They tell readers when to pause and indicate how the writer's ideas relate to one another.

30a Commas with Introductory Elements

Introductory elements such as conjunctive adverbs and introductory phrases usually need to be set off by commas.

When a conjunctive adverb or introductory phrase begins a sentence, the comma follows.

> Therefore, the suspect could not have been at the scene of the crime.

> Because cycloheximide acts on the 60S subunit of the eukaryotic ribosome, it is very toxic to people.

When a conjunctive adverb comes in the middle of a sentence, set it off with commas preceding and following.

> Ampicillin is not effective, however, against *E. coli*-BG.

Occasionally the conjunctive adverb or phrase blends into a sentence so smoothly that a pause would sound awkward.

> **Awkward** Even if you take every precaution, the pipes in your home may freeze, nevertheless.

> **Better** Even if you take every precaution, the pipes in your home may freeze nevertheless.

COMMON ERRORS

Commas with long introductory modifiers

Long subordinate clauses or phrases that begin sentences should be followed by a comma. The following sentence lacks the needed comma.

Incorrect Without the statistical background to understand and interpret them researchers find large complex data sets essentially useless.

When you read this sentence, you likely had to go back to sort it out. The words *them researchers find* tend to run together. When the comma is added, the sentence is easier to understand because the reader knows where the subordinate clause ends and where the main clause begins:

Correct Without the statistical background to understand and interpret them, researchers find large complex data sets essentially useless.

How long is a long introductory modifier? Short introductory adverbial phrases and clauses of five words or fewer can get by without the comma if the omission does not mislead the reader. Using the comma is still correct after short introductory adverbial phrases and clauses:

Correct In the long run stocks have always done better than bonds.

Correct In the long run, stocks have always done better than bonds.

Remember: Put commas after long introductory modifiers.

30b Commas with Compound Sentences

Two main clauses joined by a coordinating conjunction (*and, or, so, yet, but, nor, for*) form a compound sentence. Writers sometimes get confused about when to insert a comma before a coordinating conjunction.

COMMON ERRORS

Identifying compound sentences that require commas

The easiest way to distinguish between compound sentences and sentences with phrases that follow the main clause is to isolate the part that comes after the conjunction. If the part that follows the conjunction can stand on its own as a complete sentence, insert a comma. If it cannot, omit the comma.

Main Clause Plus Phrases

Mario thinks he lost his passport while riding the bus or by absentmindedly leaving it on the counter when he checked into the hostel.

Look at what comes after the coordinating conjunction *or:*

by absentmindedly leaving it on the counter when he checked into the hostel

This group of words is not a main clause and cannot stand on its own as a complete sentence. Do not set it off with a comma.

Main Clauses Joined with a Conjunction

On Saturday Mario went to the consulate to get a new passport, but the officer told him that replacement passports could not be issued on weekends.

Read the clause after the coordinating conjunction *but:*

the officer told him that replacement passports could not be issued on weekends

Because this group of words can stand on its own as a complete sentence, it is a main clause; place a comma before *but.*

Remember:
1. Place a comma before the coordinating conjunction (*and, but, for, or, nor, so, yet*) if there are two main clauses.
2. Do not use a comma before the coordinating conjunction if there is only one main clause.

Use a comma and a coordinating conjunction to join main clauses

Main clauses carry enough grammatical weight to be punctuated as sentences. When two main clauses are joined by a coordinating conjunction, place a comma before the coordinating conjunction in order to distinguish them.

> As the experiment continues, L-malyl-CoA decreases steadily, and both acetyl-CoA and CoA increase.

Very short main clauses joined by a coordinating conjunction do not need commas.

> She called and she called, but no one answered.

Do not use a comma to separate two verbs with the same subject

> Incorrect   Sandy borrowed two boxes full of files on Tuesday, and returned them on Friday.

Sandy is the subject of both *borrowed* and *returned*. This sentence has only one main clause; it should not be punctuated as a compound sentence.

> Correct   Sandy borrowed two boxes full of files on Tuesday and returned them on Friday.

Do not use a comma to separate a restrictive clause or phrase from a main clause

When clauses and phrases that follow the main clause are essential to the meaning of a sentence, they should not be set off with a comma.

> Incorrect   The computer and data analysis skills, that I acquired this past summer, would be helpful in the co-op portion of the degree.

> Correct   The computer and data analysis skills that I acquired this past summer would be helpful in the co-op portion of the degree.

COMMON ERRORS

Do not use a comma to set off a *because* clause that follows a main clause

Writers frequently place unnecessary commas before *because* and similar subordinate conjunctions that follow a main clause. *Because* is not a co-ordinating conjunction; thus it should not be set off by a comma unless the comma improves readability.

Incorrect The stickiness of the wet product also contributed to the lower yield, because it was impossible to get the product completely out of the reaction vial.

Correct The stickiness of the wet product also contributed to the lower yield because it was impossible to get the product completely out of the reaction vial.

But do use a comma after an introductory *because* clause.

Incorrect Because Danny left his red jersey at home the coach benched him.

Correct Because Danny left his red jersey at home, the coach benched him.

Remember: Use a comma after a *because* clause that begins a sentence. Do not use a comma to set off a *because* clause that follows a main clause.

30c Commas with Nonrestrictive Modifiers

Imagine that you are sending a friend a group photo that includes your aunt. Which sentence is correct?

In the back row the woman wearing the pink hat is my aunt.

In the back row the woman, wearing the pink hat, is my aunt.

Both sentences can be correct depending on what is in the photo. If there are three women standing in the back row and only one is wearing a pink hat, this piece of information is necessary for identifying your aunt. In this case the sentence without commas is correct because it identifies your aunt as the woman wearing the pink hat. Such necessary modifiers are **restrictive** and do not require commas.

If only one woman is standing in the back row, *wearing the pink hat* is extra information and not necessary for identifying your aunt. The modifier in this case is **nonrestrictive** and is set off by commas.

Distinguish restrictive and nonrestrictive modifiers

You can distinguish restrictive and nonrestrictive modifiers by deleting the modifier and then deciding whether the remaining sentence is changed. For example, delete the modifier *still stained by its bloody Tiananmen Square crackdown* from the following sentence:

> Some members of the Olympic Site Selection Committee wanted to prevent China, still stained by its bloody Tiananmen Square crackdown, from hosting the 2008 games.

The result leaves the meaning of the main clause unchanged.

> Some members of the Olympic Site Selection Committee wanted to prevent China from hosting the 2008 games.

The modifier is nonrestrictive and should be set off by commas.

Pay special attention to appositives

Clauses and phrases can be restrictive or nonrestrictive, depending on the context. Often the difference is obvious, but some modifiers require close consideration, especially appositives. An **appositive** is a noun or noun phrase that identifies or adds information to the noun preceding it.

Consider the following pair.

1   The best-selling vehicles SUVs usually rate the lowest on fuel efficiency.

2   The best-selling vehicles, SUVs, usually rate the lowest on fuel efficiency.

Which is correct? The appositive *SUVs* is not essential to the meaning of the sentence and offers additional information. Thus, it is a nonrestrictive appositive and should be set off with commas. Sentence 2 is correct.

Use commas to mark off parenthetical expressions

A **parenthetical expression** provides information or commentary that usually is not essential to the sentence's meaning.

Incorrect   The organelles and debris can be separated based on size using differential velocity centrifugation or by density using density gradient centrifugation.

Correct   The organelles and debris can be separated based on size, using differential velocity centrifugation, or by density, using density gradient centrifugation.

30d Commas with Items in a Series

In a series of three or more items, place a comma after each item except the last one. The comma between the last two items goes before the coordinating conjunction (*and, or, nor*).

Health officials in Trenton, Ottawa, and Thunder Bay have all reported new cases of the West Nile virus.

30e Commas with Coordinate Adjectives

Coordinate adjectives are two or more adjectives that each modify the same noun independently. Coordinate adjectives that are not linked by *and* must be separated by a comma.

After the technology bubble burst in 2000 and 2001, parents discouraged their children from careers in computer science because it was no longer the in-demand, lucrative market for graduates.

You can recognize coordinate adjectives by reversing their order; if their meaning remains the same, the adjectives are coordinate and must be linked by *and* or separated by a comma.

Commas are not used between **cumulative adjectives**. Cumulative adjectives are two or more adjectives that work together to modify a noun: *deep blue sea, inexpensive mountain bike*. If reversing their order changes the description of the noun (or violates the word order of English, such as *mountain inexpensive bike*), the adjectives are cumulative and should not be separated by a comma.

30f Commas with Quotations

Properly punctuating quotations with commas can be tricky unless you know a few rules about when and where to use commas.

When to use commas with quotations

Commas set off phrases that attribute quotations to a speaker or writer, such as *he argues, they said,* and *she writes.*

> "When you come to a fork in the road," said Yogi Berra, "take it!"

If the attribution follows a quotation that is a complete sentence, replace the period that normally would come at the end of the quotation with a comma.

Incorrect	"I believe in good omens. I don't believe in the bad ones." notes Silken Laumann.
Correct	"I believe in good omens. I don't believe in the bad ones," notes Silken Laumann.

When an attribution is placed in the middle of a quotation, put the comma preceding the attribution within the quotation mark just before the phrase.

When not to use commas with quotations

Do not replace a question mark or exclamation point with a comma, and do not add a comma after a question mark or an exclamation point.

Incorrect	"Who's in the playoffs," John asked rhetorically.
Correct	"Who's in the playoffs?" John asked rhetorically.

Not all phrases that mention the author's name are attributions. When quoting a term or using a quotation within a subordinate clause, do not set off the quotation with commas.

"Stonewall" Jackson gained his nickname at the First Battle of Bull Run when General Barnard Bee shouted to his men that Jackson was "standing like a stone wall."

Commas with Dates, Numbers, Titles, and Addresses

Some of the easiest comma rules to remember are the ones we use every day in dates, numbers, personal titles, place names, direct address, and brief interjections.

Commas with dates

Use commas to separate the day of the week from the month and to set off a year from the rest of the sentence.

Monday, November 18, 2014

On February 12, 2010, the opening ceremony for the Olympic Games was televised from Vancouver, B.C.

Do not use a comma when the month immediately precedes the year.

April 2015

Commas with numbers

Commas mark off thousands, millions, billions, and so on.

16,500,000

However, do not use commas in street addresses or page numbers.

page 1542

7602 Yonge Street

Commas with personal titles

When a title follows a person's name, set the title off with commas.

Frederick Banting, MD

Commas with place names

Place a comma between street addresses, city names, provinces, and countries.

The prime minister lives at 24 Sussex Drive, Ottawa, Ontario.

Commas with brief interjections

Use commas to set off brief interjections like *yes* and *no,* as well as short questions that fall at the ends of sentences.

Have another piece of pie, won't you?

30h Commas to Avoid Confusion

Certain sentences can confuse readers if you do not indicate where they should pause within the sentence. Use a comma to guide a reader through these usually compact constructions.

Unclear   With supplies low prices of gasoline and fuel oil will increase.

This sentence could be read as meaning *With supplies, low prices will increase.*

Clear   With supplies low, prices of gasoline and fuel oil will increase.

30i Unnecessary Commas

Do not place a comma between a subject and the main verb.

Incorrect   Canadian children of immigrant parents, often do not speak their parents' native language.

Correct   Canadian children of immigrant parents often do not speak their parents' native language.

However, you do use commas to set off modifying phrases that separate subjects from verbs.

Correct   Gilles Duceppe, leader of the Bloc Québécois, inadvertently alienated many Quebec voters in the 2011 election.

Do not use a comma with a coordinating conjunction unless it joins two main clauses. (See the Common Errors box on page 242.)

Incorrect   Susana thought finishing her first novel was hard, but soon learned that getting a publisher to buy it was much harder.

Correct   Susana thought finishing her first novel was hard but soon learned that getting a publisher to buy it was much harder.

Correct   Susana thought finishing her first novel was hard, but she soon learned that getting a publisher to buy it was much harder.

Do not use a comma after a subordinating conjunction such as *although, despite,* or *while.*

Incorrect   Although, soccer is gaining popularity in Canada, it will never be as popular as football or hockey.

Correct   Although soccer is gaining popularity in Canada, it will never be as popular as football or hockey.

Some writers mistakenly use a comma with *than* to try to heighten the contrast in a comparison.

Incorrect   Any teacher will tell you that acquiring critical thinking skills is more important, than simply memorizing information.

Correct   Any teacher will tell you that acquiring critical thinking skills is more important than simply memorizing information.

A common mistake is to place a comma after *such as* or *like* before introducing a list.

Incorrect	Many hourly workers, such as, waiters, dishwashers, and cashiers, do not receive dental benefits from their employers.
Correct	Many hourly workers, such as waiters, dishwashers, and cashiers, do not receive dental benefits from their employers.

31 | Semicolons and Colons

QUICK*TAKE*

- Use semicolons to link related ideas (see below)
- Use colons correctly in sentences and lists (see pp. 253–255)

31a Semicolons with Closely Related Main Clauses

Why use semicolons? Sometimes you want to join two main clauses to indicate their close relationship. You can connect them with a comma and a coordinating conjunction like *or, but,* or *and.* But to create variation in sentence style and avoid wordiness, just insert a semicolon between the two clauses.

Semicolons can join only clauses that are grammatically equal. In other words, they join main clauses to other main clauses, not to phrases or subordinate clauses. Look at the following examples:

Incorrect	┌─────────── MAIN CLAUSE ───────────┐ Gloria's new weightlifting program will help her recover └──────────┘ ┌──── PARTICIPAL PHRASE ────┐ from knee surgery; doing a series of squats and presses └────┘ with a physical therapist.
Correct	┌─────────── MAIN CLAUSE ───────────┐ Gloria's new weightlifting program will help her recover └──────────┘ ┌──── MAIN CLAUSE ────┐ from knee surgery; a physical therapist leads her through └────────────┘ a series of squats and presses.

Do not use a semicolon to introduce quotations

Use a comma or colon instead.

Incorrect Pauline Johnson's poem "Canadian Born" opens with these lines; "We first saw light in Canada, the land be-loved of God / We are the pulse of Canada, its marrow and its blood."

Correct Pauline Johnson's poem "Canadian Born" opens with these lines: "We first saw light in Canada, the land be-loved of God / We are the pulse of Canada, its marrow and its blood."

COMMON ERRORS

Semicolons with transitional words and phrases

Closely related main clauses sometimes use a conjunctive adverb (such as *however, therefore, moreover, furthermore, thus, meanwhile, nonetheless, otherwise*) or a transitional phrase (*in fact, for example, that is, for instance, in addition, in other words, on the other hand, even so*) to indicate the relationship between them. When the second clause begins with a conjunctive adverb or a transitional phrase, a semicolon is needed to join the two clauses. This sentence pattern is frequently used; therefore, it pays to learn how to punctuate it correctly.

Incorrect
(comma splice) No one doubts that exercise burns calories, however, few people can lose weight by exercise alone.

Correct No one doubts that exercise burns calories; however, few people can lose weight by exercise alone.

Remember: Two main clauses joined by a conjunctive adverb or a transitional phrase require a semicolon.

Do not use a semicolon to introduce lists

Incorrect   William Shakespeare wrote four romance plays at the end of his career; *The Tempest, The Winter's Tale, Cymbeline,* and *Pericles.*

Correct   William Shakespeare wrote four romance plays at the end of his career: *The Tempest, The Winter's Tale, Cymbeline,* and *Pericles.*

31b Semicolons Together with Commas

When an item in a series already includes a comma, adding more commas to separate it from the other items will only confuse the reader. Use semicolons instead of commas between items in a series that have internal punctuation.

Confusing   The church's design competition drew entries from as far away as Gothenberg, Sweden, Caracas, Venezuela, and Athens, Greece.

Clearer   The church's design competition drew entries from as far away as Gothenberg, Sweden; Caracas, Venezuela; and Athens, Greece.

31c Colons in Sentences

Like semicolons, colons can join two closely related main clauses (complete sentences). Colons indicate that what follows will explain or expand on what comes before the colon. Use a colon in cases where the second main clause interprets or sums up the first.

Internet retailers have a limited customer base: only those who have Internet access can become e-shoppers.

You may choose to capitalize the first word of the main clause following the colon or leave it lowercase. Either is correct as long as you are consistent throughout your text.

Colons linking main clauses with appositives

A colon calls attention to an appositive, a noun, or a noun phrase that re-names the noun preceding it. If you're not certain whether a colon would be appropriate, put *namely* in its place. If *namely* makes sense when you read the main clause followed by the appositive, you probably need to in-sert a colon instead of a comma. Remember, the clause that precedes the colon must be a complete sentence.

Test for correctness   I know the perfect person for the job, namely me.

The sentence makes sense with *namely* placed before the appositive. Thus, a colon is appropriate.

Correct   I know the perfect person for the job: me.

Never capitalize a word following a colon unless the word starts a complete sentence or is normally capitalized.

Colons joining main clauses with quotations

Use a colon to link a main clause and a quotation that interprets or sums up the clause. Be careful that the clause introducing the colon and quota-tion is a complete sentence.

Incorrect: Noun Phrase–Colon–Quotation

Jacques Cartier's first encounter with the land that would be Canada: "I am rather inclined," he confessed, "to believe that this is the land God gave to Cain."

Correct: Main Clause–Colon–Quotation

Jacques Cartier's first encounter with the land that would be Canada was not promising: "I am rather inclined," he confessed, "to believe that this is the land God gave to Cain."

The first example is incorrect because there is no main verb in the first part of the sentence and thus it is a phrase rather than a main clause. The sec-ond example adds the verb (*was*) to complete the thought, making the first part of the sentence a main clause.

 **Colons with Lists**

Use a colon to join a main clause to a list. The main clauses in these cases sometimes include the phrases *the following* or *as follows*. Remember that what precedes the colon should be a complete sentence.

Incorrect: Noun Phrase–Colon–List

Three posters decorating Jacques' apartment: an old Santana concert poster, a view of Grouse Mountain, and a Diego Rivera mural.

Correct: Main Clause–Colon–List

Jacques bought three posters to decorate his apartment: an old Santana concert poster, a view of Grouse Mountain, and a Diego Rivera mural.

COMMON ERRORS

Colons misused with lists

Some writers think that anytime they introduce a list, they should insert a colon. Colons are used correctly only when a complete sentence precedes the colon.

Incorrect	The topics sought for the journal include: communications technologies, readability of communication materials, and social impact of communications.
Correct	The topics sought for the journal include communications technologies, readability of communication materials, and social impact of communications.
Correct	The topics sought for the journal include the following: communication technologies, readability of communication materials, and social impact of communication.

Remember: A colon should be placed only after a clause that can stand by itself as a sentence.

32 Dashes and Parentheses

QUICK*TAKE*

- Use dashes and parentheses rather than commas to set off information (see below)
- Use other punctuation correctly with parentheses (see p. 259)

Dashes and parentheses can be excellent tools for setting off and calling attention to information that comments on your ideas. They serve as visual cues to the reader of a sudden break in thought or change in sentence structure. Note that dashes (formed with two hyphens or the em-dash character in a word processor) and hyphens are not the same. **Hyphens** punctuate words; **dashes** punctuate sentences.

Dashes and Parentheses to Set off Information

Dashes and parentheses call attention to groups of words. In effect, they tell the reader that a group of words is not part of the main clause and should be given extra attention. If you want to make an element stand out, especially in the middle of a sentence, use parentheses or dashes instead of commas.

Dashes with final elements

A dash is often used to set off a phrase or subordinate clause at the end of a sentence to offer a significant comment about the main clause. Dashes can also anticipate a shift in tone at the end of a sentence.

A full-sized SUV can take you wherever you want to go in style—if your idea of style is a gas-guzzling tank.

Parentheses with additional information

Parentheses are more often used for identifying information, afterthoughts or asides, examples, and clarifications. You can place full sentences, fragments, or brief terms within parentheses.

Normalizing the values allowed us to retrieve a brightness parameter independent of time (see insert in Figure 6).

32b Dashes and Parentheses Versus Commas

Like commas, parentheses and dashes enclose material that adds, explains, or digresses. However, the three punctuation marks are not interchangeable. The mark you choose depends on how much emphasis you want to place on the material. Dashes indicate the most emphasis. Parentheses offer somewhat less, and commas offer less still.

Commas Indicate a Moderate Level of Emphasis

By 2030 more than one billion people, mainly from the developing world, will join the "global middle class."

COMMON ERRORS

Do not use dashes as periods

Do not use dashes to separate two main clauses (clauses that can stand as complete sentences). Use dashes to separate main clauses from subordinate clauses and phrases when you want to emphasize the subordinate clause or phrase.

Incorrect: Main Clause–Dash–Main Clause

I was one of the few women in my computer science classes—most of the students majoring in computer science at that time were men.

Correct: Main Clause–Dash–Phrase

I was one of the few women in computer science—a field then dominated by men.

Remember: Dashes are not periods and should not be used as periods.

Parentheses Lend a Greater Level of Emphasis

How have Canadian ideas of place and belonging been shaped by the Charter of Rights and Freedoms (30 years has passed since its ratification)?

Dashes Indicate the Highest Level of Emphasis and, Sometimes, Surprise or Drama

bell hooks asks a compelling question: "Can we embrace an ethos of sustainability that is not solely about the appropriate care of the world's resources, but is also about the creation of meaning—the making of lives that we feel are worth living?"

COMMON ERRORS

The art of typing a dash

Although dashes and hyphens may look similar, they are different marks. The distinction is important because dashes and hyphens serve different purposes. A dash is a line much longer than a hyphen. Most software will create a dash automatically when you type two hyphens together.

Do not leave a space between a dash or a hyphen and the words that come before and after them. Likewise, if you are using two hyphens to indicate a dash, do not leave a space between the hyphens.

Incorrect   A well - timed effort at conserving water may prevent long - term damage to drought - stricken farms - - if it's not already too late.

Correct   A well-timed effort at conserving water may prevent long-term damage to drought-stricken farms—if it's not already too late.

Remember: Do not put spaces before or after hyphens and dashes.

32c Other Punctuation with Parentheses

Parentheses around letters or numbers that order a series within a sentence make the list easier to read.

> Angela Creider's recipe for becoming a great novelist is to (1) set aside an hour during the morning to write, (2) read out loud what you've written, (3) revise your prose, and (4) repeat every morning for the next thirty years.

COMMON ERRORS

Using periods, commas, colons, and semicolons with parentheses

When an entire sentence is enclosed in parentheses, place the period before the closing parenthesis.

Incorrect   Our fear of sharks, heightened by movies like *Jaws,* is vastly out of proportion with the minor threat sharks actually pose. (Dying from a dog attack, in fact, is much more likely than dying from a shark attack).

Correct   Our fear of sharks, heightened by movies like *Jaws,* is vastly out of proportion with the minor threat sharks actually pose. (Dying from a dog attack, in fact, is much more likely than dying from a shark attack.)

When the material in parentheses is part of the sentence and the parentheses fall at the end of the sentence, place the period outside the closing parenthesis.

Incorrect   Reports of sharks attacking people are rare (much rarer than dog attacks.)

Correct   Reports of sharks attacking people are rare (much rarer than dog attacks).

Place commas, colons, and semicolons after the closing parenthesis.

Remember: When an entire sentence is enclosed in parentheses, place the period inside the closing parenthesis; otherwise, put the punctuation outside the closing parenthesis.

Abbreviations made from the first letters of words are often used in place of the unwieldy names of institutions, departments, organizations, or terms. To show the reader what the abbreviation stands for, the first time it appears in a text the writer should state the complete name, followed by the abbreviation in parentheses.

> The University of California, Santa Cruz (UCSC) supports its mascot, the banana slug, with pride and a sense of humour. And although it sounds strange to outsiders, UCSC students are even referred to as "the banana slugs."

33 | Apostrophes

QUICKTAKE

- Use apostrophes to show possession (see below)
- Use apostrophes to show omitted letters (see p. 262)

33a Possessives

Nouns and indefinite pronouns (for example, *everyone, anyone*) that indicate possession or ownership are marked by attaching an apostrophe and an *s* or an apostrophe only to the end of the word.

Singular nouns and indefinite pronouns

For singular nouns and indefinite pronouns, add an apostrophe plus *s*: instructor's. Even singular nouns that end in *s* usually follow this principle.

> Iris's coat
>
> everyone's favourite
>
> a woman's choice

There are a few exceptions to adding *'s* for singular nouns:

Official names of certain places, institutions, companies: *Loblaws, Staples, KidsAbility-Centre for Child Development.* Note, however, that many companies do include the apostrophe: *Denny's Restaurant, Shopper's Drug Mart, McDonald's, Wendy's Old Fashioned Hamburgers.*

Plural nouns

For plural nouns that do not end in *s*, add an apostrophe plus *s*:

media's responsibility

children's section

For plural nouns that end in *s*, add only an apostrophe at the end.

attorneys' briefs

the Trudeaus' legacy

Compound nouns

For compound nouns, add an apostrophe plus *s* to the last word of the compound noun: *-'s.*

premier-elect's speech

Two or more nouns

For joint possession, add an apostrophe plus *s* to the final noun: *-'s.*

Mom and Dad's yard

When people possess or own things separately, add an apostrophe plus *s* to each noun:

Roberto's and Edward's views are totally opposed.

COMMON ERRORS

Possessive forms of personal pronouns never take the apostrophe

Incorrect	*her's, it's, our's, your's, their's*
	The bird sang in **it's** cage.
Correct	*hers, its, ours, yours, theirs*
	The bird sang in **its** cage.

Remember: It's = It is

33b   Contractions and Omitted Letters

In speech we often leave out sounds and syllables of familiar words. These omissions are noted with apostrophes.

Contractions

Contractions combine two words into one, using the apostrophe to mark what is left out.

I am	⟶	I'm	we are	⟶	we're
you are	⟶	you're	they are	⟶	they're
you will	⟶	you'll	cannot	⟶	can't
he is	⟶	he's	do not	⟶	don't
she is	⟶	she's	does not	⟶	doesn't
it is	⟶	it's	will not	⟶	won't

Omissions

Using apostrophes to signal omitted letters is a way of approximating speech in writing. They can make your writing look informal and slangy, and overuse can become annoying in a hurry.

rock and roll	⟶	rock 'n' roll
neighbourhood	⟶	'hood

Plurals of Letters, Symbols, and Words Referred to as Words

When to use apostrophes to make plurals

The trend is away from using apostrophes to form plurals of letters, symbols, and words referred to as words. Most readers now prefer 1960s to the older form, 1960's. In a few cases adding the apostrophe and *s* is still used, as in this old saying:

Mind your p's and q's.

Words used as words are italicized and their plural formed by adding an *s* not in italics, instead of an apostrophe and *s*.

Take a few of the *and*s out of your writing.

When not to use apostrophes to make plurals

Do not use an apostrophe to make family names plural.

Incorrect   You've heard of keeping up with the Jones's.

Correct   You've heard of keeping up with the Joneses.

COMMON ERRORS

Do not use an apostrophe to make a noun plural

Incorrect   The two government's agreed to meet.

Correct   The two governments agreed to meet.

Remember:
Add only *s* = plural
Add apostrophe plus *s* = possessive

34 Quotation Marks

QUICK_TAKE_

- Correctly incorporate words from sources (see below)
- Use quotation marks correctly with other punctuation (see p. 266)

34a Direct Quotations

Use quotation marks to enclose direct quotations

Enclose direct quotations—someone else's words repeated verbatim—in quotation marks.

> Anne Lamott advises writers to look at everything with compassion, even something as seemingly inconsequential as a chipmunk: "I don't want to sound too Cosmica Rama here, but in those moments, you see that you and the chipmunk are alike, are part of a whole" (98).

Do not use quotation marks with indirect quotations

Do not enclose an indirect quotation—a paraphrase of someone else's words—in quotation marks. However, do remember that you need to cite your source not only when you quote directly but also when you paraphrase or borrow ideas.

> Anne Lamott encourages writers to become compassionate observers who ultimately see themselves as equals to everything else, even something as seemingly inconsequential as a chipmunk (98).

Do not use quotation marks with block quotations

When a quotation is long enough to be set off as a block quotation, do not use quotation marks. MLA style defines long quotations as five or more lines; APA style defines a long quotation as one of more than 40 words.

In the following example, notice that the long quotation is indented and quotation marks are omitted. Also notice that the parenthetical citation for a long quotation comes after the period.

> Complaints about maintenance in residence have been on the rise ever since the physical plant reorganized its crews into teams in August. One student's experience is typical:
>> When our ceiling started dripping, my roommate and I went to our floor don right away to file an emergency maintenance request. By the fourth day without any word from a maintenance person, the ceiling tiles began to fall and puddles began to pool on our carpet. (Albertson)

34b Titles of Short Works

While the titles of longer works such as books, magazines, and newspapers are italicized or underlined, titles of shorter works should be set off with quotation marks. Use quotation marks with the following kinds of titles:

Short Stories	"Boys and Girls," by Alice Munro
Magazine Articles	"Born Again in Syria," by Michael Petrou
Newspaper Articles	"Stamp Auction Revives Canada's Postal Scandal," by Randy Boswell
Short Poems	"We Real Cool," by Gwendolyn Brooks
Essays	"Self-Reliance," by Ralph Waldo Emerson

The exception. Don't put the title of your own paper in quotation marks. If the title of another short work appears within the title of your paper, retain the quotation marks around the short work.

34c Other Uses of Quotation Marks

Quotation marks around a term can indicate that the writer is using the term in a novel way, often with skepticism, irony, or sarcasm: *How is your "pet" spider today?* The quotation marks indicate that the writer is questioning the term's definition.

Italics are usually used to indicate that a word is being used as a word, rather than standing for its conventional meaning. However, quotation marks are correct in these cases as well.

Beginning writers sometimes confuse "their," "they're," and "there."

COMMON ERRORS

Quotations within quotations

Single quotation marks are used to indicate a quotation within a quotation. In the following example single quotation marks clarify who is speaking. The rules for placing punctuation with single quotation marks are the same as the rules for placing punctuation with double quotation marks.

Incorrect   When he showed the report to Paul Probius, Michener reported that Probius "took vigorous exception to the sentence "He wanted to close down the university," insisting that we add the clarifying phrase "as it then existed"" (Michener 145).

Correct   When he showed the report to Paul Probius, Michener reported that Probius "took vigorous exception to the sentence 'He wanted to close down the university,' insisting that we add the clarifying phrase 'as it then existed'" (Michener 145).

Remember: Single quotation marks are used for quotations within quotations.

34d Other Punctuation with Quotation Marks

The rules for placing punctuation with quotation marks fall into three general categories.

Periods and commas with quotation marks

Place periods and commas inside closing quotation marks.

Incorrect	"The smartest people", Dr. Geisler pointed out, "tell themselves the most convincing rationalizations".
Correct	"The smartest people," Dr. Geisler pointed out, "tell themselves the most convincing rationalizations."

Colons and semicolons with quotation marks

Place colons and semicolons outside closing quotation marks.

Incorrect	"From Stettin in the Baltic to Trieste in the Adriatic, an iron curtain has descended across the Continent;" Churchill's statement rang through Cold War politics for the next fifty years.
Correct	"From Stettin in the Baltic to Trieste in the Adriatic, an iron curtain has descended across the Continent"; Churchill's statement rang through Cold War politics for the next fifty years.

Exclamation points, question marks, and dashes with quotation marks

When an exclamation point, question mark, or dash belongs to the original quotation, place it inside the closing quotation mark. When it applies to the entire sentence, place it outside the closing quotation mark.

In The Original Quotation

"Are we there yet?" came the whine from the back seat.

Applied to The Entire Sentence

Did the driver in the front seat respond, "Not even close"?

34e Misuses of Quotation Marks

It's becoming more and more common to see quotation marks used to emphasize a word or phrase. Resist the temptation in your own writing; the usage is incorrect. In fact, because quotation marks indicate that a writer is using a term with skepticism or irony, adding quotation marks for emphasis will highlight unintended connotations of the term.

Incorrect "fresh" seafood

By using quotation marks here, the writer seems to call into question whether the seafood is really fresh.

Correct fresh seafood

Incorrect Enjoy our "live" music every Saturday night.

Again, the quotation marks unintentionally indicate that the writer is skeptical that the music is live.

Correct Enjoy our live music every Saturday night.

35 | Other Punctuation Marks

QUICK*TAKE*

- Use periods, question marks, and exclamation points correctly (see below, and pp. 269–271)
- Use brackets and ellipses correctly (see pp. 271–272)

 Periods

Periods at the ends of sentences

Place a period at the end of a complete sentence if it is not a direct question or an exclamatory statement.

Periods with quotation marks and parentheses

When a quotation falls at the end of a sentence, place the period inside the closing quotation marks.

> Although he devoted decades to a wide range of artistic and political projects, Allen Ginsberg is best known as the author of the poem "Howl."

When a parenthetical phrase falls at the end of a sentence, place the period outside the closing parenthesis. When parentheses enclose a whole sentence, place the period inside the closing parenthesis.

Periods with abbreviations

Many abbreviations require periods; however, there are few set rules. Use the dictionary to check how to punctuate abbreviations on a case-by-case basis. The rules for punctuating two types of abbreviations do remain consistent: postal abbreviations and most abbreviations for organizations do not require periods. When an abbreviation with a period falls at the end of a sentence, do not add a second period to conclude the sentence.

Incorrect	Her flight arrives at 6:22 p.m..
Correct	Her flight arrives at 6:22 p.m.

Periods as decimal points

Decimal points are periods that separate integers from tenths, hundredths, and so on.

99.98% pure silver   98.6° Fahrenheit
on sale for $399.97   2.6 litre engine

35b Question Marks

Question marks with direct questions

Place a question mark at the end of a direct question. A direct question is one that the questioner puts to someone outright. In contrast, an indirect question merely reports the asking of a question. Question marks give readers a cue to read the end of the sentence with rising inflection. Read the following sentences aloud. Hear how your inflection rises in the second sentence to convey the direct question.

Indirect Question

Desirée asked whether Dan rides his motorcycle without a helmet.

Direct Question

Desirée asked, "Does Dan ride his motorcycle without a helmet?"

Question marks with quotations

When a quotation falls at the end of a direct question, place the question mark outside the closing quotation mark.

> Did Brian Mulroney really say, "My father dreamed of a better life for his family. I dream of a better life for my country"?

Place the question mark inside the closing quotation when only the quoted material is a direct question.

> Slowly scientists are beginning to answer the question, "Is cancer a genetic disease?"

When quoting a direct question in the middle of a sentence, place a question mark inside the closing quotation mark and place a period at the end of the sentence.

> Market researchers estimate that asking Burger World's customers "Do you want fries with that?" is responsible for a 15% boost in french fries sales.

35c Exclamation Points

Exclamation points to convey strong emotion

Exclamation points conclude sentences and, like question marks, tell the reader how a sentence should sound. They indicate strong emotion. Use exclamation points sparingly in formal writing; they are rarely appropriate in academic and professional prose.

Exclamation points with emphatic interjections

Exclamation points can convey a sense of urgency with brief interjections. Interjections can be incorporated into sentences or stand on their own.

> Run! They're about to close the doors to the jetway.

Exclamation points with quotation marks

In quotations, exclamation points follow the same rules as question marks. If a quotation falls at the end of an exclamatory statement, place the exclamation point outside the closing quotation mark.

The singer forgot the words to "O Canada"!

When quoting an exclamatory statement at the end of a sentence that is not itself exclamatory, place the exclamation point inside the closing quotation mark.

Jerry thought his car would be washed away in the flood, but Anna jumped into action, declaring, "Not if I can help it!"

35d Brackets

While brackets (sometimes called *square brackets*) look quite similar to parentheses, the two perform different functions. Brackets have a narrow set of uses.

Brackets to provide clarification within quotation marks

Use brackets if you are interjecting a comment of your own or clarifying information within a direct quotation. In the following example the writer quotes a sentence with the pronoun *they*, which refers to a noun in a previous, unquoted sentence. The material in brackets clarifies to whom the pronoun refers.

The Harris study found that "In the last three years, they [Pauline Johnson Senior Public School students] averaged 15% higher on their mathematics assessment tests than their peers at Father Breboeuf."

Brackets within parentheses

Since parentheses within parentheses might confuse readers, use brackets to enclose parenthetical information within a parenthetical phrase.

Representative Patel's most controversial legislation (including a version of the hate crimes bill [HR 99-108] the legislature rejected two years ago) has a slim chance of being enacted this session.

35e Ellipses

Ellipses let a reader know that a portion of a passage is missing. You can use ellipses to keep quotations concise and direct readers' attention to what

is important to the point you are making. An ellipsis is a string of three periods with spaces separating the periods.

Ellipses to indicate an omission from a quotation

When you quote only a phrase or short clause from a sentence, you usually do not need to use ellipses.

> Mao Zedong first used "let a hundred flowers blossom" in a Beijing speech in 1957.

Except at the beginning of a quotation, indicate omitted words with an ellipsis.

> "The female praying mantis . . . tears off her male partner's head during mating."

When the ellipsis is at the end of a sentence, place the period or question mark after the ellipsis and follow with the closing quotation mark.

Words Omitted at The End of a Sentence

> "This brutal dance is a stark example of the innate evolutionary drive to pass genes on to offspring. . . ."

36 | Capitalization, Italics, Abbreviations, Numbers

QUICKTAKE

- Capitalize words properly (see below)
- Use italics correctly (see p. 273)
- Use abbreviations correctly (see p. 273)

36a Capital Letters

Capitalize the initial letters of proper nouns (nouns that name particular people, places, and things). Capitalize the initial letters of proper adjectives (adjectives based on the names of people, places, and things).

Afro-Caribbean bookstore   Avogadro's number   Irish music

Do not capitalize the names of seasons, academic disciplines (unless they are languages), or job titles used without a proper noun.

36b Italics

Italicize the titles of entire works (books, magazines, newspapers, films), but place the titles of parts of entire works within quotation marks. When italicizing is difficult because you are writing by hand, underline the titles of entire works instead. Also italicize or underline the names of ships and aircraft.

I am fond of reading the *Star Phoenix* in the morning.

Exception: Do not italicize or underline the names of sacred texts.

Italicize unfamiliar foreign words

Italicize foreign words that are not part of common English usage. Do not italicize words that have become a common word or phrase in the English vocabulary. How do you decide which words are common? If a word appears in a standard English dictionary, it can be considered as adopted into English.

status quo

Use italics to clarify your use of a word, letter, or number

In everyday speech, we often use cues—a pause, a louder or different tone—to communicate how we are using a word. In writing, italics help clarify when you use words in a referential manner, or letters and numbers as letters and numbers.

Please list your first choice as *one*.

36c Abbreviations

Abbreviations are shortened forms of words. Because abbreviations vary widely, you will need to look in the dictionary to determine how to abbreviate words on a case-by-case basis. Nonetheless, there are a few patterns that abbreviations follow.

Abbreviate titles before and degrees after full names

Ms. Rita MacNeil, P.Eng.

Prof. Vijay Aggarwal, Ph.D.

Spell out the professional title when it is used with only a last name.

Professor Chin

Reverend Ames

Conventions for using abbreviations with years and times

BCE (before the common era) and CE (common era) are now preferred for indicating years, replacing BC (before Christ) and AD (*anno Domini* ["the year of our Lord"]). Note that all are now used without periods.

479 BCE (or BC)

1610 CE (or AD 1610)

The preferred written conventions for times are a.m. (*ante meridiem*) and p.m. (*post meridiem*).

9:03 a.m.

3:30 p.m.

Latin abbreviations

Some writers sprinkle Latin abbreviations throughout their writing, apparently thinking them a mark of learning. Frequently these abbreviations are used inappropriately. If you use Latin abbreviations, make sure you know what they stand for.

e.g. (*exempli gratia*) or for example
et al. (*et alia*) or and others
etc. (*et cetera*) or and so forth
i.e. (*id est*) or that is
NB (*nota bene*) or note well

In particular, avoid using *etc.* to fill out a list of items. Use of *etc.* announces that you haven't taken the time to finish a thought.

Lazy	The contents of his grocery cart described his eating habits: a big bag of chips, hot sauce, frozen pizza, **etc.**
Better	The contents of his grocery cart described his eating habits: a big bag of chips, a large jar of hot sauce, two frozen pizzas, a twelve-pack of cola, three Mars bars, and a package of Twinkies.

Conventions for using abbreviations in post-secondary writing

Most abbreviations are inappropriate in formal writing except when the reader would be more familiar with the abbreviation than with the words it represents. When your reader is unlikely to be familiar with an abbreviation, spell out the term, followed by the abbreviation in parentheses, the first time you use it in a paper. The reader will then understand what the abbreviation refers to, and you may use the abbreviation in subsequent sentences.

The Toronto Stock Exchange (TSX) posted record high gains today.

36d Acronyms

Acronyms are abbreviations formed by capitalizing the first letter in each word. Unlike other abbreviations, acronyms are pronounced as words.

AIDS for Acquired Immunodeficiency Syndrome

NASA for National Aeronautics and Space Administration

Many initial-letter abbreviations (not pronounced as words) have become so common that we know the organization or thing by its initials.

OPP for Ontario Provincial Police

HIV for human immunodeficiency virus

rpm for revolutions per minute

Familiar initial-letter abbreviations such as CBC, CIBC, FBI, IQ, and UN are rarely spelled out. Unfamiliar acronyms and abbreviations should always be spelled out. Abbreviations frequent in particular fields should be spelled out on first use. For example, MMPI (Minnesota Multiphasic Personality Inventory) is a familiar abbreviation in psychology but is unfamiliar to those outside that discipline. Even when abbreviations are generally familiar, few readers will object to your spelling out the words on the first use.

36e Numbers

In formal writing spell out any number that can be expressed in one or two words, as well as any number, regardless of length, at the beginning of a sentence. Also, hyphenate two-word numbers from twenty-one to ninety-nine. When a sentence begins with a number that consists of more than two words, revise it if possible.

The exceptions: In scientific reports and some business writing that requires the frequent use of numbers, using numerals more often is appropriate. Most styles do not write out in words a year, a date, an address, a page number, the time of day, decimals, sums of money, phone numbers, rates of speed, or the scene and act of a play. Use numerals instead.

In 2001 only 33% of respondents said they were satisfied with the City Council's proposals to help the homeless.

The 17 trials were conducted at temperatures of 12-14°C with results ranging from 2.43 to 2.89 mg/dl.

When one number modifies another number, write one out and express the other in numeral form.

In the last year all four 8th Street restaurants have begun to donate their leftovers to the soup kitchen.

Only after Meryl had run in 12 fifty-mile ultramarathons did she finally win first place in her age group.

Glossary of Grammatical Terms and Usage

The glossary gives the definitions of grammatical terms and items of usage. The grammatical terms are shown in blue. Some of the explanations of usage that follow are not rules, but guidelines to keep in mind for academic and professional writing. In these formal contexts, the safest course is to avoid words that are described as *nonstandard, informal,* or *colloquial.*

a/an   Use *a* before words that begin with a consonant sound (*a train, a house*). Use *an* before words that begin with a vowel sound (*an airplane, an hour*).

a lot/alot   *A lot* is generally regarded as informal; *alot* is incorrect.

accept/except   *Accept* is a verb meaning "receive" or "approve"; *except* is sometimes a verb meaning "leave out," but much more often it's used as a conjunction or preposition meaning "other than."

active voice   A clause with a transitive verb in which the subject is the doer of the action (see Section 19a). See also passive voice.

adjective   A modifier that qualifies or describes the qualities of a noun or pronoun (see Sections 28a and b).

adverb   A word that modifies a verb, another modifier, or a clause (see Sections 28a and c).

adverb clause   A subordinate clause that functions as an adverb by modifying a verb, another modifier, or a clause (see Section 28c).

advice/advise   The noun *advice* means a "suggestion"; the verb *advise* means to "recommend" or "give advice."

affect/effect   Usually, *affect* is a verb (to "influence") and *effect* is a noun (a "result"). Less commonly, *affect* is used as a noun and *effect* as a verb.

agreement   The requirement that the number and person of a subject and verb must match—singular subjects with singular verbs, plural subjects with plural verbs (see Chapter 24). Likewise, the number and gender of a pronoun and its antecedent must match (see Section 26c).

all ready/already   The adjective phrase *all ready* means "completely prepared"; the adverb *already* means "previously."

all right/alright   *All right,* meaning "acceptable," is the correct spelling. *Alright* is nonstandard.

allude/elude   *Allude* means "refer to indirectly." *Elude* means "evade."

allusion/illusion   An *allusion* is an indirect reference; an *illusion* is a false impression.

among/between   *Between* refers to precisely two people or things; *among* refers to three or more.

amount/number   Use *amount* with things that cannot be counted; use *number* with things that can be counted.

an   See **a/an.**

antecedent   The noun (or pronoun) that a pronoun refers to (see Section 26b).

anybody/any body; anyone/any one   *Anybody* and *anyone* are indefinite pronouns and have the same meaning; *any body* and *any one* are usually followed by a noun that they modify.

anymore/any more   *Anymore* means "now," while *any more* means "no more." Both are used in negative constructions.

anyway/anyways   *Anyway* is correct; *anyways* is nonstandard.

articles   The words *a*, *an*, and *the* (see Section 29b).

as/as if/as though/like   Use *as*, *as if*, or *as though* instead of *like* before dependent clauses (which include a subject and verb). Use *like* before a noun or a pronoun.

assure/ensure/insure   *Assure* means "promise," *ensure* means "make certain," and *insure* means to "make certain in either a legal or financial sense."

auxiliary verb   Forms of *be, do,* and *have* combine with verbs to indicate tense and mood (see Section 29c). The modal verbs *can, could, may, might, must, shall, should, will,* and *would* are a subset of auxiliaries.

bad/badly   Use *bad* only as an adjective. *Badly* is the adverb.

being as/being that   Both constructions are colloquial and awkward substitutes for *because*. Don't use them in formal writing.

beside/besides   *Beside* means "next to." *Besides* means "in addition to" or "except."

between   See **among/between.**

bring/take   *Bring* describes movement from a more distant location to a nearer one. *Take* describes movement away.

can/may   In formal writing, *can* indicates ability or capacity, while *may* indicates permission.

case   The form of a noun or pronoun that indicates its function. Nouns change case only to show possession: the *dog*, the *dog's* bowl. See also pronoun case (see also Section 26a).

censor/censure   To *censor* is to edit or ban on moral or political grounds; to *censure* is to reprimand publicly.

cite/sight/site   To *cite* is to "mention specifically"; *sight* as a verb means to "observe" and as a noun refers to "vision"; *site* is most commonly used as a noun that means "location," but it is also used as a verb to mean "situate."

clause   A group of words with a subject and a predicate. A main or independent clause can stand as a sentence. A subordinate or dependent clause must be attached to a main clause to form a sentence (see Section 23a).

collective noun   A noun that refers to a group or a plurality, such as *team, army,* or *committee* (see Section 24d).

comma splice   Two independent clauses joined incorrectly by a comma (see Section 23c).

common noun   A noun that names a general group, person, place, or thing (see Section 29a). Common nouns are not capitalized unless they begin a sentence. See also proper noun.

complement   A word or group of words that completes the predicate. See also linking verb.

complement/compliment   To *complement* something is to complete it or make it perfect; to *compliment* is to flatter.

complex sentence   A sentence that contains at least one subordinate clause attached to a main clause.

compound sentence   A sentence that contains at least two main clauses.

compound-complex sentence   A sentence that contains at least two main clauses and one subordinate clause.

conjunction   See coordinating conjunction and subordinating conjunction.

conjunctive adverb   An adverb that often modifies entire clauses and sentences, such as *also, consequently, however, indeed, instead, moreover, nevertheless, otherwise, similarly,* and *therefore* (see Section 28c).

continual/continuous   *Continual* refers to a repeated activity; *continuous* refers to an ongoing, unceasing activity.

coordinate   A relationship of equal importance, in terms of either grammar or meaning (see Section 21c).

coordinating conjunction   A word that links two equivalent grammatical elements, such as *and, but, or, yet, nor, for,* and *so.*

could of   Nonstandard. See **have/of**.

count noun   A noun that names things that can be counted, such as *block, cat,* and *toy* (see Section 29a).

dangling modifier   A modifier that is not clearly attached to what it modifies (see Section 28e).

data   The plural form of *datum;* it takes plural verb forms.

declarative   A sentence that makes a statement.

dependent clause   See subordinate clause.

determiners   Words that initiate noun phrases, including possessive nouns (*Pedro's violin*); possessive pronouns (*my, your*); demonstrative pronouns (*this, that*); and indefinite pronouns (*all, both, many*).

differ from/differ with   To *differ from* means to "be unlike"; to *differ with* means to "disagree."

different from/different than   Use *different from* where possible. *Dark French roast is different from ordinary coffee.*

direct object   A noun, pronoun, or noun clause that names who or what receives the action of a transitive verb.

discreet/discrete   Both are adjectives. *Discreet* means "prudent" or "tactful"; *discrete* means "separate."

disinterested/uninterested   *Disinterested* is often misused to mean *uninterested*. *Disinterested* means "impartial." *A judge can be interested in a case but disinterested in the outcome.*

double negative   The incorrect use of two negatives to signal a negative meaning.

due to the fact that   Avoid this wordy substitute for *because*.

each other/one another   Use *each other* for two; use *one another* for more than two.

effect   See **affect/effect**.

elicit/illicit   The verb *elicit* means to "draw out"; the adjective *illicit* means "unlawful."

emigrate from/immigrate to   *Emigrate* means to "leave one's country"; *immigrate* means to "settle in another country."

ensure   See **assure/ensure/insure**.

enthused   Nonstandard in academic and professional writing. Use *enthusiastic* instead.

etc.   Avoid this abbreviation for the Latin *et cetera* in formal writing. Either list all the items or use an English phrase such as *and so forth*.

every body/everybody; every one/everyone   *Everybody* and *everyone* are indefinite pronouns referring to all people under discussion. *Every one* and *every body* are adjective-noun combinations referring to all members of a group.

except   See **accept/except**.

except for the fact that   Avoid this wordy substitute for *except that*.

expletive   The dummy subjects *it* and *there* used to fill a grammatical slot in a sentence. *It is raining outside. There should be a law against it.*

explicit/implicit   Both are adjectives; *explicit* means "stated outright," while *implicit* means just the opposite, "unstated."

farther/further   *Farther* refers to physical distance; *further* refers to time or other abstract concepts.

fewer/less   Use *fewer* with what can be counted and *less* with what cannot be counted.

flunk   In formal writing, avoid this colloquial substitute for *fail.*

fragment   A group of words beginning with a capital letter and ending with a period that looks like a sentence but lacks a subject or a predicate or both (see Section 23a).

further   See **farther/further.**

gerund   An *-ing* form of a verb used as a noun, such as *running, skiing,* or *laughing.*

good/well   *Good* is an adjective and is not interchangeable with the adverb *well.* The one exception is health. Both *she feels good* and *she feels well* are correct.

hanged/hung   Use *hanged* to refer only to executions; use *hung* for all other instances.

have/of   *Have,* not *of,* follows *should, could, would, may, must,* and *might.*

he/she; s/he   Try to avoid language that appears to exclude either gender (unless this is intended, of course) and awkward compromises such as *he/she* or *s/he.* The best solution is to make pronouns plural (the gender-neutral *they*) wherever possible (see Section 26c).

helping verb   See auxiliary verb.

hopefully   This adverb is commonly used as a sentence modifier, but many readers object to it.

illusion   See **allusion/illusion.**

immigrate   See **emigrate from/immigrate to.**

imperative   A sentence that expresses a command. Usually the subject is implied rather than stated.

implicit   See **explicit/implicit.**

imply/infer   *Imply* means to "suggest"; *infer* means to "draw a conclusion."

in regards to   Avoid this wordy substitute for *regarding.*

incredible/incredulous   *Incredible* means "unbelievable"; *incredulous* means "not believing."

independent clause   See main clause.

indirect object   A noun, pronoun, or noun clause that names who or what is affected by the action of a transitive verb.

infinitive   The word *to* plus the base verb form: *to believe, to feel, to act.*

infinitive phrase   A phrase that uses the infinitive form of a verb.

interjection   A word expressing feeling that is grammatically unconnected to a sentence, such as *cool, wow, ouch,* or *yikes.*

interrogative   A sentence that asks a question.

intransitive verb   A verb that does not take an object, such as *sleep, appear,* or *laugh* (see Sections 25c and 29c).

irregardless   Nonstandard for *regardless*.

irregular verb   A verb that does not use either *-d* or *-ed* to form the past tense and past participle (see Section 25b).

it is my opinion that   Avoid this wordy substitute for *I believe that.*

its/it's   *Its* is the possessive of *it* and does not take an apostrophe; *it's* is the contraction for *it is.*

-ize/-wise   The suffix *-ize* changes a noun or adjective into a verb (*harmony, harmonize*). The suffix *-wise* changes a noun or adjective into an adverb (*clock, clockwise*). Some writers are tempted to use these suffixes to convert almost any word into an adverb or verb form. Unless the word appears in a dictionary, don't use it.

kind of/sort of/type of   Avoid using these colloquial expressions when you mean *somewhat* or *rather*. *It's kind of hot* is nonstandard. Each is permissible, however, when it refers to a classification of an object. Be sure that it agrees in number with the object it is modifying.

lay/lie   *Lay* means "place" or "put" and generally takes a direct object (see Section 000). Its main forms are *lay, laid, laid*. *Lie* means "recline" or "be positioned" and does not take an object. Its main forms are *lie, lay, lain.*

less   See **fewer**.

lie   See **lay/lie**.

linking verb   A verb that connects the subject to the complement, such as *appear, be, feel, look, seem,* or *taste.*

lots/lots of   Nonstandard in formal writing; use *many* or *much* instead.

main clause   A group of words with a subject and a predicate that can stand alone as a sentence; also called an *independent clause.*

mankind   This term offends some readers and is outdated. Use *humans, humanity, humankind,* or *people* instead.

may/can   See **can/may**.

may be/maybe   *May be* is a verb phrase; *maybe* is an adverb.

media   This is the plural form of the noun *medium* and requires a plural verb.

might of   See **have/of**.

modal   A kind of auxiliary verb that indicates ability, permission, intention, obligation, or probability, such as *can, could, may, might, must, shall, should, will,* or *would.*

modifier   A general term for adjectives, adverbs, phrases, and clauses that describe other words (see Chapter 28).

must of   See **have/of.**

noncount noun   A noun that names things that cannot be counted, such as *air, energy,* or *water* (see Section 29a).

nonrestrictive modifier   A modifier that is not essential to the meaning of the word, phrase, or clause it modifies; it should be set off by commas or other punctuation (see Section 30c).

noun   The name of a person, place, thing, concept, or action. See also common noun and proper noun (see Section 29a).

noun clause   A subordinate clause that functions as a noun.

number   See **amount/number.**

object   Receiver of the action within the clause or phrase.

OK, O.K., okay   Informal; avoid using in academic and professional writing. Each spelling is accepted in informal usage.

owing to the fact that   Avoid this wordy, colloquial substitute for *because.*

parallelism   The principle of putting similar elements or ideas in similar grammatical form (see Section 21c).

participial phrase   A phrase formed either by a present participle (for example, *racing*) or by a past participle (for example, *taken*).

participle   A form of a verb that uses -*ing* in the present (*laughing, playing*) and usually -*ed* or -*en* in the past (*laughed, played*); see Section 25a. Participles are either part of the verb phrase (*She had played the game before*) or used as adjectives (*the laughing girl*).

parts of speech   The eight classes of words grouped by their grammatical function: nouns, pronouns, verbs, adjectives, adverbs, prepositions, conjunctions, and interjections.

passive voice   A clause with a transitive verb in which the subject is being acted upon (see Section 19a). See also active voice.

people/persons   *People* refers to a general group; *persons* refers to a collection of individuals. Use *people* over *persons* except when you're emphasizing the idea of separate persons within the group.

per   Try to use the English equivalent of this Latin word except in technical writing or familiar usages like *miles per gallon.*

phenomena   The plural form of *phenomenon* ("observable fact" or "unusual event"); it takes a plural verb.

phrase   A group of words that does not contain both a subject and predicate.

plenty   In academic and professional writing, avoid this colloquial substitute for *very*.

plus   Do not use *plus* to join clauses or sentences. Use *and, also, moreover, furthermore,* or another conjunctive adverb instead.

precede/proceed   Both are verbs, but they have different meanings: *precede* means "come before," and *proceed* means "go ahead" or "continue."

predicate   The part of the clause that expresses the action or tells something about the subject. The predicate includes the verb and all its complements, objects, and modifiers.

prejudice/prejudiced   *Prejudice* is a noun; *prejudiced* is an adjective.

preposition   A class of words that indicate relationships and qualities.

prepositional phrase   A phrase formed by a preposition and its object, including the modifiers of its object.

pronoun   A word that stands for other pronouns or nouns. Pronouns have several subclasses, including personal pronouns, possessive pronouns, demonstrative pronouns, indefinite pronouns, relative pronouns, interrogative pronouns, reflexive pronouns, and reciprocal pronouns (see Chapter 26).

pronoun case   Pronouns that function as the subjects of sentences are in the **subjective** case (*I, you, he, she, it, we, they*). Pronouns that function as direct or indirect objects are in the **objective** case (*me, you, him, her, it, us, them*). Pronouns that indicate ownership are in the **possessive** case (*my, your, his, her, its, our, their*) (see Section 26a).

proper noun   A noun that names a particular person, place, thing, or group (see Section 29a). Proper nouns are capitalized.

question as to whether/question of whether   Avoid these wordy substitutes for *whether*.

raise/rise   The verb *raise* means "lift up" and takes a direct object. Its main forms are *raise, raised, raised.* The verb *rise* means "get up" and does not take a direct object. Its main forms are *rise, rose, risen.*

real/really   Avoid using *real* as if it were an adverb. *Really* is an adverb; *real* is an adjective.

reason is because   Omit either *reason is* or *because* when explaining causality.

reason why   Avoid using this redundant combination.

relative pronoun   A pronoun that initiates clauses, such as *that, which, what, who, whom,* or *whose.*

restrictive modifier   A modifier that is essential to the meaning of the word, phrase, or clause it modifies (see Section 30c). Restrictive modifiers are usually not set off by punctuation.

rise/raise   See **raise/rise.**

run-on sentence   Two main clauses fused together without punctuation or a conjunction, appearing as one sentence (see Section 23b).

sentence   A grammatically independent group of words that contains at least one main clause.

sentence fragment   See **fragment**.

shall/will   *Shall* is used most often in first person questions, while *will* is a future tense helping verb for all persons. British English consistently uses *shall* with first person: *I shall, we shall.*

should of   See **have/of**.

some time/sometime/sometimes   *Some time* means "a span of time," *sometime* means "at some unspecified time," and *sometimes* means "occasionally."

somebody/some body; someone/some one   *Somebody* and *someone* are indefinite pronouns and have the same meaning. In *some body, body* is a noun modified by *some,* and in *some one, one* is a pronoun or adjective modified by *some.*

sort of   See **kind of/sort of/type of**.

stationary/stationery   *Stationary* means "motionless"; *stationery* means "writing paper."

subject   A noun, pronoun, or noun phrase that identifies what the clause is about and connects with the predicate.

subject-verb agreement   See **agreement**.

subordinate   A relationship of unequal importance, in terms of either grammar or meaning (see Section 21a).

subordinate clause   A clause that cannot stand alone but must be attached to a main clause; also called a *dependent clause.*

subordinating conjunction   A word that introduces a subordinate clause. Common subordinating conjunctions are *after, although, as, because, before, if, since, that, unless, until, when, where,* and *while.*

such   Avoid using *such* as a synonym for *very.* It should always be followed by a *that* and a clause that contains a result.

sure   A colloquial term used as an adverb to mean "certainly." Avoid using it this way in formal writing.

sure and/sure to; try and/try to   *Sure to* and *try to* are correct; do not use *and* after *sure* or *try.*

take   See **bring/take**.

that/which   *That* introduces a restrictive or essential clause. Restrictive clauses describe an object that must be that particular object and no other. Though some writers occasionally use *which* with restrictive clauses, it is most often used to introduce nonrestrictive clauses. These are clauses that contain additional nonessential information about the object.

transition   A word or phrase that notes movement from one unit of writing to another.

transitive verb   A verb that takes a direct object (see Section 25c).

verb   A word that expresses action or characterizes the subject in some way. Verbs can show tense and mood (see Chapter 25 and Section 29c).

verbal   A form of a verb used as an adjective, adverb, or noun. See also gerund, infinitive, participle.

well/good   See **good/well**.

which/that   See **that/which**.

who/whom   *Who* and *whom* follow the same rules as other pronouns: *Who* is the subject pronoun; *whom* is the object pronoun (see Section 26a).

will/shall   See **shall/will**.

-wise/-ize   See **-ize/-wise**.

would of   See **have/of**.

you   Avoid indefinite uses of *you*. It should only be used to mean "you, the reader."

your/you're   The two are not interchangeable. *Your* is the possessive form of "you"; *you're* is the contraction of "you are."

Index

K

key verbs, 8
keywords
  defined, 30
  identifying, 47–48
  search for, 47
keyword search engines, 54–55
kind of/sort of/type of, 282

L

lab report
  conclusion and discussion
    of, 24
  elements of, 23–24
  writing, 23–24
language
  inclusive, 31
  specific, 31, 195
lay/lie, 215, 282
less/fewer, 281
letters
  abbreviations and first, 260
  capital, 272–273
  to editor, 96, 97
  omitted, 262
  plural, 263
LexisNexis Academic, 53, 79
library
  catalogue of, 46
  online sources of, 41, 46
Library and Archives
  Canada, 55
library database sources
  citation in, 49–50
  legal case from, 102
  MLA-style in-text citation
    and, 91–92, 102
  newspaper articles from, 102
  online, 41, 46
  visuals and, 55–56
  Web sources *vs.,* 59–60
library print sources
  audio, 46
  citation in, 51–52
  documentaries as, 46
  finding, 48–49
  government publication as,
    46, 105, 133
  identifying keywords in,
    47–48
  maps as, 46

MLA-style in-text citation
    and, 95–98
  reliability of, 58–59
  trade journals as, 46
  types of sources within, 46
  video as, 46
  working bibliography as, 45
lie/lay, 282
like/as/as if/as though, 250, 278
limiting modifiers, 231
linkage
  back to front, 188–189
  front to front, 187–188
linking paragraph, 14
linking verbs, 282
links
  between claim and reason, 16
  between paragraph, 31
  to reports, 172
  across sentences, 187–189
lists
  colons with, 255
  discussion, 105–106,
    153–154
  semicolon and, 253
literary works, 86
long introductory modifiers, 241
lots/lots of, 282

M

magazines
  see also journals; periodical
    sources
  articles from, 102
  bi-weekly or weekly, 96,
    150–151
  CMS-style bibliography and,
    96, 150–151
  CMS-style note and, 96,
    150–151
  government publication, 46,
    105, 133
  MLA-style in-text citation
    and, 95–98
  monthly or seasonal, 95
  online, 132
  popular, 46, 104
main clauses, 255, 257
  adverbs and second, 230
  adverbs between two, 230
  with appositives and
    colons, 254

because clause following, 244
  comma separating, 243
  with conjunction, 242
  defined, 282
  main ideas in, 186
  into phrase, 206
  plus phrase, 242
  with quotations and colons,
    254
  relationship between,
    203–204
  restrictive clause or phrase
    and, 243
  semicolon with, 251–253
  into subjective clause, 206
mankind, 282
maps, 37–39, 46, 56, 107
materials. *See* methods and
  materials
may be/maybe, 282
may/can, 278
me, 35
meaning, 68, 238
mechanics, 31
media, 282
methods and materials, 11, 24
might of. See have/of
MLA documentation, 74–75
  block quotations in, 71
  citation of sources in, 76–78
  formatting for, 108–109
  in-text citations, 81–87
    see also MLA-style in-text
      citation
  sample research paper with,
    108–109
  works-cited list. *See* MLA-style
    works-cited list
*MLA Handbook for Writers of
  Research Papers,* seventh
  edition (2009), 76
MLA-style in-text citation
  afterword, foreword,
    introduction or preface
    and, 100
  anthology and, 85, 100
  author's name and, 77, 79,
    83–85, 91–92, 94, 97
  different authors with same
    last name and, 85
  editor and, 89–90
  formatting for, 108–109

introduction and, 100
journals, magazines, newspapers, other print sources
and, 95–98
library database sources and,
91–92, 102
literary works and, 86
online sources (citation) and,
86, 93–94
for paraphrase and summary,
77–78, 81–82
printed books and, 89–90
publisher and, 90
quotations and, 76–77,
81–82, 84
on reviews, 96
sample, 83–86
two or more sources within
same citation and, 85
two or more works by same
author and, 85
unnamed authors and, 84
visual sources and, 106–107
work by four or more authors
and, 83
work by group or organization
and, 84, 99
work by one author and, 83
work by two or three authors
and, 83
work quoted in another source
and, 85
*MLA Style Manual and Guide to
Scholarly Publishing*, third
edition (2008), 76
MLA-style works-cited list
author's name and, 49–52
creation of, 78–80
formatting for, 109
online sources (citation) and,
49–52
periodicals and, 87–88
religious texts and, 100
sample of, 87–94
sample research paper and,
110–116
modal, 237, 282
Modern Language Association
(MLA). *See* MLA docu-
mentation
modifiers
see also adjectives; adverbs

absolute, 229
comma with nonrestrictive,
244–246
comparative or correct,
227–228
dangling, 232–233, 279
defined, 283
hyphens with compound,
231–232
introductory, 240
limiting, 231
long introductory, 241
nonrestrictive, 244–246, 283
restrictive, 245, 284
superlative, 227–228
varieties of, 227
words and, 233
monthly or seasonal
magazines, 95
mood, in shifts, 225
multilingual speakers,
233–238
multimedia genres, 1, 27–29
multimedia projects
audio production as, 29
creating, 27–29
essay with images and visuals
as, 27–29
oral presentation as, 27
video production as, 29
multimedia sources, 86
see also database sources;
online sources
in APA-style references list,
133
online, 55–57
must of. See have/of

N

narration
books with graphic, 101
descriptions in, 24, 29
necessity, 237
neither . . . nor, 208
nervousness, 36
newspaper articles
APA-style in-text citation
and, 128
authors of, 97
CMS-style bibliography and,
151
CMS-style note and, 151

continuance of nonconsecutive page within, 97
from library database sources,
102
online, 132
on Web, 104
newspapers
MLA-style in-text citation
and, 95–98
name of, 88
reviews of, 97
sources for, 46
noncount noun, 234, 236, 283
nonnative speakers
articles, noun, verbs and,
234–238
common ESL errors of, 234,
236
grammar for, 233–238
nonperiodical sources
APA-style references list and,
122–125
CMS-style bibliography and,
143–147
CMS-style note and,
143–147
CSE-style in-text citations
and, 160–162
nonrestrictive modifiers,
244–246, 283
nonstandard words, 277
notes, 142, 146–148
noun, 231
apostrophes and compound,
261
apostrophes and plural, 261,
263
apostrophes and singular, 260
apostrophes and two or more,
261
clause, 283
collective, 220, 279
common, 234, 279
count, 234, 236, 279
defined, 283
noncount, 234, 236, 283
nonnative and multilingual
speakers and, 234–238
proper, 232, 234, 284
subject-verb agreement with
another, 208
subject with another, 208

Credits

The publisher wishes to thank the following sources for photographs, illustrations, and other materials used in this book. Care has been taken to determine and locate ownership of copyright material used in this text. We will gladly receive information enabling us to rectify any errors or omissions in credits.

TEXT

p. 20, Sample Observation excerpt from student essay. Reprinted with permission of Erin Graves.

p. 28, Sara Macdonald's Holy Cow (2002). London: Bantam.

p. 66, Jeff Speck, *Walkable City: How Downtown Can Save America One Step at a Time.* New York: Farrar, 2012. Print.

pp. 68, 69, Steven Johnson, *Interface Culture: How New Technology Transforms the Way We Create and Communicate.* (New York: Harper, 1997), 107–109.

p. 71, Ulysses S. Grant, *Personal memories of U.S. Grant.* (New York: C.L. Webster), 68.

p. 72, Michael Lewis, *Next: The Future Just Happened.* (New York: W.W. Norton & Company Ltd.), 14.

p. 77, Claeys, Gregory, "The Origins of Dystopia: Wells, Huxley and Orwell." *The Cambridge Companion to Utopian Literature.* Ed. Gregory Claeys. Cambridge UP, 2010. Cambridge Collections Online. Web. 6 Mar. 2012.

p. 78, Christopher S. Ferns, *Narrating Utopia: Ideology, Gender, Form in Utopian Literature.* (Liverpool University Press, 1999).

pp. 81, 82, Janet Giltrow, "Curious Gentlemen": The Hudson's Bay Company and the Royal Society, Business and Science in the Eighteenth Century.

p. 84, "Art for Everybody" by Susan Orlean, *The New Yorker,* October 15, 2001. p. 128.

p. 86 Andrew Keen, "Blogs are Boring," May 23, 2007.

p. 86, Miguel De Cervantes, *Don Quixote,* translated by Edith Grossman, Harper Perennial, 2005.

p. 93, Theresa Hyland, "Multilingual Learners in the Writing Centre: Some Musings on Negotiated Practice." *Inkshed* 31 (January 2014). Web. 4 April 2014.

p. 110, Student Essay: "Satiric Dystopia in The Time Machine and We," Matt Loicano. Reprinted with permission of Eric Graves.

p. 188, S. Zukin, *Point of purchase: How shopping changed American culture.* (New York: Routledge, 2004).

p. 134, Student Essay: "How the Media Depict Nursing Impacts Stereotypes and Nursing Practice," Danielle Mitchell.

p. 142, Alison Prentice et al., *Canadian Women: A History* (Toronto: Harcourt Brace Jovanovich, 1988), 93.

p. 155, Student essay: "Love and Marriage in the Works of Elizabeth Cary and Lady Mary Wroth" by Elizabeth Moore. Reprinted with permission of C.A. Chambers.

p. 189, Nellie McClung.

p. 197, *The Publication Manual of the American Psychological Association,* 5th ed.

p. 236, Max Anikovsky, Zach D. Wiltshire, Klaus Weisshart, and Nils O. Petersen, "Photon Counting Histogram Analysis for Two-Dimensional Systems,"*Biophysical Journal* (Impact Factor: 3.83). 01/2013; 104(2).

p. 247, Yogi Berra, *When You Come to a Fork in the Road, Take It!: Inspiration and Wisdom From One of Baseball's Greatest Heroes* (Hyperion, 2002).

p. 247, Silken Laumann.

p. 252, Emily Pauline Johnson.

p. 254, Jacques Cartier.

p. 256, Bell Hooks, *Belonging: A Culture of Place* (New York: Routledge, 2009).

p. 264, Anne Lamott, *Bird by Bird: Some Instructions on Writing and Life* (Anchor Books, 1995), 98.

p. 272, Mao Zedong as quoted in Harry Wu; Hongda Harry Wu; George Vecsey (30 December 2002). "Troublemaker: One Man's Crusade Against China's Cruelty." NewsMax Media, Inc. pp. 49–55.

IMAGES

p. 1, Part 1 and all pages in part with tab images, Rorouge/Fotolia; p. 7, Steven Frame/Shutterstock; p. 33, The Writing Process, © Pearson Education, Inc.; p. 33, light bulb, Dr. Cloud/Shutterstock; p. 33, 2 figures, Higyou/Shutterstock; p. 33, magnifying glass, Dip/Shutterstock; p. 33, sheet of paper, Pearson Education, Inc.; p. 35, Zhu Difeng/Shutterstock; p. 37, Part 2 and all pages in part with tab images, Mikenorton/Shutterstock; p. 73, Part 3, Ahturner/Shutterstock; pp. 76, 78, Cambridge Collections Online. Reprinted with the permission of Cambridge University Press.; p. 87, *Ecological Applications*. Online by Ecological Society of America. Reproduced with permission of Ecological Society of America in the format Republish in a book via Copyright Clearance Center.; p. 89, University of Alberta Press; p. 91, Reprinted by permission of ProQuest LLC.; p. 93, Inkshed; p. 122, From *Cad Monkeys, Dinosaur Babies, and T-Shaped People: Inside the World of Design Thinking and How It Can Spark Creativity and Innovation* by Warren Berger, copyright © 2009 by Warren Berger. Used by permission of Penguin, a division of Penguin Group (USA) LLC.; p. 126, © Pearson Education, Inc.; p. 129 Tenenbaum, D. J. (2005). "Global warming: Arctic climate: The heat is on." *Environmental Health Perspectives*, 113, A91. http://dx.doi.org/:10.1289/ehp.113-a91a; p. 143, From *Big Bear* by Rudy Wiebe. Copyright © Jackpine House Ltd., 2008. Reprinted by permission of Penguin Canada Books Inc.; p. 151, Cover page and copyright page of "Recovery Strategy for the Piping Plover (Charadrius melodus melodus) in Canada," Species at Risk Act: Recovery Strategy Series. Environment Canada. © Her Majesty the Queen in Right of Canada, represented by the Minister of the Environment, 2012. Environment Canada Permissions, N/A; p. 155, Chardine photography/John Chardine; p. 160, David W. Schindler & John R. Vallentyne, *The Algal Bowl: Overfertilization of the World's Freshwatersand Estuaries.* The University of Alberta Press (2008). Used by permission.; p. 163, Applied physics letters by American Institute of Physics. Reproduced with permission of American Institute of Physics. In the format reprint in a book/ebook via Copyright Clearance Center.; p. 169, M. McCool, "Information architecture: Intercultural human factors," *Tech. Commun.,* vol. 53, no. 2, pp. 167–183, May 2006.; p. 172, http://www.ec.gc.ca/scitech/default.asp?lang=En&n=AC4418A5-1; p. 173, J. Wells, Cover page of "Assessment of the environmental Performance of Solar Photovoltaic Technologies," Minister of the Environment, Cat. No. En84-88/2012E (2012) http://www.ec.gc.ca/scitech/B53B14DE-034C-457B-8B2B-39AFCFED04E6/ForContractor_721_Solar_Photovoltaic_Technology_e_09%20FINAL-update%202-s.pdf, Environment Canada Permissions; p. 175, Part 4 and all pages in part with tab images, Alexey Fedoren/Fotolia; p. 176, top, Samot/Shutterstock; p. 176, bottom, Ronald Karpilo/Alamy; p. 180, Tinatin/Fotolia; p. 185, top left, jbor/Shutterstock; p. 185, top right, Banana Republic images/Shutterstock; p. 185, bottom, Glenn W. Walker/Shutterstock; p. 199, Part 5 and all pages in part with tab images, Viparat Kluengsuwanchai/123RF; p. 239, Part 6 and all pages in part with tab images, Santi Rodriguez/Fotolia; Common Error box art, Konstantin Faraktinov/Shutterstock; Box photo, Ammentorp Photography/Shutterstock; Cover, Theseamuss/Fotolia.

NOTES

NOTES